SLIPS, TRIPS, AND FALLS IN NEW MEXICO

A 505 LEGAL GUIDE

KENNETH H. STALTER

Published by Stalter Law LLC, a subsidiary of 505 Legal, P.C.
PO Box 90336, Albuquerque, NM 87199
www.505legal.com

Library of Congress Cataloging-in-Publication Data
Stalter, Kenneth H.
Slips, Trips, and Falls in New Mexico: A 505 Legal Guide / Kenneth H. Stalter
ISBN: 979-8-9928381-4-5

Printed in the United States of America
First Edition: 2026

Also by Kenneth H. Stalter

Beyond Your Release Date: Fighting Illegal Detention in New Mexico's Prisons and Jails

Follow the Money with New Mexico Public Records: A 505 Legal Guide

New Mexico Car Accident Claims: A 505 Legal Guide

Dedicated to the clients who trusted me with their cases. You taught me more than you know.

CONTENTS

ABOUT 505 LEGAL

505 Legal was co-founded by Farmington criminal defense attorney Shellie Patscheck and Albuquerque insurance attorney Kenneth Stalter because we saw a problem in New Mexico.

Communities across the state—especially outside the big metro areas—were losing attorneys. The traditional hometown lawyer, the person you could turn to when legal trouble found you, was disappearing. But we also recognized the limits of that traditional model: the solo generalist, pulled in too many directions, often lacked the depth that serious cases require.

We wanted to build something different. A modern hometown law firm that uses contemporary tools and systems to deliver focused expertise—while maintaining the accessibility and community roots that made hometown lawyers valuable. A top-notch, local legal team rather than a single overwhelmed attorney.

Too many people encounter the legal system on one of the worst days of their lives. They then find themselves overwhelmed by noise, pressure, and half-truths.

We believe informed clients make better decisions, even when those decisions are difficult. We believe people should be participants in their cases, not passengers. And we believe good legal work is measured not by slogans or verdict headlines, but by whether the outcome serves the client's goals.

ABOUT 505 LEGAL GUIDES

Publishing plain-English legal guides is part of our mission at 505 Legal.

We want the people we serve to understand the processes they're facing—not because understanding replaces professional help, but because it makes professional help work better. An informed client asks better questions, spots problems earlier, and makes decisions with confidence.

These guides cover legal topics that matter to everyday New Mexicans. Each one is written for people with no legal background, focused on practical steps rather than theory. The goal is always the same: to turn readers into active participants in their own cases.

We hope you'll choose 505 Legal when you need an attorney. But even if you don't, we hope these guides help you wherever you go.

ABOUT THE AUTHOR

Kenneth H. Stalter was born in Albuquerque and returned to New Mexico after graduating from Harvard Law School. He has worked on both sides of the courtroom—as a prosecutor handling felony trials, as general counsel for the New Mexico Attorney General's Office, and now as co-founder of 505 Legal.

His current practice focuses on civil litigation, with an emphasis on injury and insurance claims, civil rights, and government accountability. He also holds a master's degree in cybersecurity, which informs his approach to the increasingly data-driven systems that shape modern insurance practices.

He wrote this book because he believes injured people deserve to understand the process they're facing. The insurance system isn't designed to explain itself to you. This guide is.

A FEW IMPORTANT NOTES

This book provides general information about slip, trip, and fall claims in New Mexico. It is not legal advice for your specific situation.

Every case is different. Legal rules change. The same rule can apply differently depending on the facts involved. Nothing in this book can account for every scenario you might face.

Reading this book does not create an attorney-client relationship between you and the author or 505 Legal. It does not make Kenneth Stalter your lawyer.

This book is meant to help you work more effectively with an attorney, not to replace one. The legal system is complex, insurance companies are sophisticated, and the stakes in an injury claim are real. For most people, professional help is essential.

If you've been injured in a slip, trip, or fall in New Mexico, consult a qualified attorney about your specific circumstances. Use this book to prepare for that conversation, understand the process, and participate actively in your own case.

INTRODUCTION

If you're reading this, chances are you or someone you love has been hurt in a fall. Maybe at a grocery store. Maybe at a restaurant. Maybe on a broken sidewalk or in a parking lot. You're facing a process you didn't ask for and probably don't understand. You want to know what happens next.

Maybe you're still in pain weeks after the incident. Maybe you're missing work while medical bills pile up. Maybe someone from the property owner's insurance company has called, asking questions that make you feel less like a victim and more like a suspect.

That last part catches people off guard. You fell in a national chain store—a company worth billions of dollars. You were hurt because of a hazard they failed to address. You assumed they'd make it right. Isn't that what insurance is for?

Instead, you find yourself answering questions about your shoes. About whether you were looking at your phone. About whether you've ever fallen before. About your medical history going back years. The adjuster is polite, but something feels wrong. You came into this conversation as someone who was injured. Now you feel like you're being interrogated.

Here's what most people don't realize until they're in the middle of it: the system isn't designed to help you.

That's not cynicism. It's just how the business works. Many insurance companies are corporations with shareholders expecting returns. Their adjusters are evaluated on how efficiently they close files—not on whether injured people feel whole at the end. The property owner's insurance company has no legal duty to you. Their obligation runs to their customer, the business that pays their premiums. Their job is to resolve your claim for as little as possible.

And in premises cases, they have a built-in advantage. Unlike car accidents—where fault is often clear from a police report—fall cases are murkier. The insurance company will almost always argue that you share responsibility. You should have been watching where you were going. You should have seen the hazard. Your shoes weren't appropriate. You were distracted.

These arguments have traction. Juries hear them and sometimes agree. The insurance company knows this, and they use it to push down the value of your claim—or deny it entirely.

Meanwhile, the injury law industry isn't always helping.

Flip through late-night television or drive down the interstate and you'll see what passes for attorney advertising: promises of millions, aggressive slogans, faces on billboards. What those ads don't tell you is how those firms actually operate.

Some are case mills. They sign up as many clients as possible, then hand files off to paralegals and junior staff. You might never speak to the attorney whose face is on the billboard. Your case becomes a number in a system optimized for volume, not outcomes.

This is a particular problem for premises cases. Most of those high-volume firms built their systems around car accidents—a relatively standardized case type where liability is often clear and the process is more predictable. Premises cases are different. They're more varied, more nuanced, more dependent on context. Who owns the property? Who operates it? Who maintains it? What standard of care applies to this particular type of business? Was notice required? These questions don't fit neatly into a system designed to process fender-benders.

If the firm you're talking to handles mostly auto accidents and treats your fall case as just another file in the queue, exercise caution. You may need someone who understands the specific challenges premises cases present.

Some firms settle everything quickly—not because fast settlements serve their clients, but because quick turnover means more fees with less work. Insurance companies know which attorneys will take the first reasonable offer and which ones will actually prepare for trial. They adjust their behavior accordingly.

Others overpromise. They tell you your case is worth far more than any reasonable evaluation would support, then blame the insurance company or the jury when reality arrives. You spend months or years expecting a windfall that was never realistic.

None of this serves you. The insurance company wants to pay you less. Some attorneys want to process you faster. And you're caught in the middle, trying to recover from an injury while navigating a system that wasn't built with your interests in mind.

This book exists because you deserve better.

A Different Approach

At 505 Legal, we believe the attorney-client relationship should be a partnership, not a transaction.

That means we want informed clients—people who understand what's happening in their cases and why. We don't think knowledge is something to hoard. The more you understand, the better decisions you'll make, and the more effectively we can work together.

It also means we're honest about expectations. We're not going to tell you your case is worth a million dollars to get you to sign a retainer. We're going to tell you what we actually think, based on experience, even when that's not what you want to hear. Fairness is our goal—not maximizing a number at any cost.

Our approach to claims reflects this philosophy. We're methodical. Every step of the process—identifying responsible parties, gathering evidence, working with experts, building the demand package, negotiating or litigating—gets handled deliberately, not frantically. We communicate throughout, because you shouldn't have to wonder what's happening with your own case.

We think of ourselves as a modern hometown law firm. We use today's technology, systems, and insights to deliver the kind of focused expertise that a traditional small-town generalist couldn't provide—while maintaining the accessibility and community focus that made hometown lawyers valuable in the first place. You get a local legal team, not a single overwhelmed attorney juggling too many practice areas.

That's what 505 Legal is about. And that's why we publish guides like this one.

What This Book Will Do

This book walks you through the slip, trip, and fall claims process in New Mexico—from understanding why these cases are different, to finding and working with an attorney, to navigating the complexities of liability, evidence, settlement, and litigation.

By the end, you'll understand the landscape. You'll know what questions to ask. You'll be able to spot problems early and understand the decisions that arise along the way.

You'll be equipped to participate actively in your own case—not as a lawyer, but as an informed person who understands what's happening and why.

How to Use This Book

This is a reference, not a novel. Not every chapter will apply to your situation. Use the book however it's useful.

If you want a comprehensive view of what to expect from beginning to end, read straight through.

If you've just been injured and want to know what to do right now, start with Chapter 1. It covers the immediate steps that matter most.

If you're trying to figure out whether you need an attorney, Chapter 4 walks you through that decision. If you've already decided to hire someone and want to know what to look for, skip to Chapter 5.

If you want to understand the unique challenges of premises cases—why they're harder than car accidents, why liability is often contested—Chapter 2 explains what you're up against.

If you're trying to understand what your case might be worth, Chapter 15 covers how premises claims are valued. Chapter 16 walks through how settlement negotiations actually work.

If your fall happened on government property—a city sidewalk, a state building, a public school—Chapter 11 explains the special rules that apply.

If you're feeling out of the loop with your attorney—or wondering whether the relationship is working—Chapter 7 covers what you should expect and how to raise concerns.

Skim through to get a feel for the process. Read the chapters that address your immediate questions. Skip what doesn't apply. Return to specific sections as your case progresses and new issues arise.

The goal isn't to turn you into a lawyer. It's to turn you into an informed participant.

PART 1

GETTING THE RIGHT HELP

A fall can happen in seconds. The process that follows can take months or years.

This part of the book is about building the foundation. What you do in the days after a fall matters. Who you hire matters. How you set up the working relationship with your attorney matters. Get these things right and you position yourself for the best possible outcome. Get them wrong and you're fighting uphill from the start.

The chapters ahead cover what to do immediately after a fall, why premises cases are different from other injury claims, how to find the right attorney, what fee agreements really mean, and how to make the attorney-client relationship work. By the time you finish Part I, you'll be ready to work alongside your legal team as an informed partner.

Part II gets into the nuts and bolts—how liability works, how to preserve evidence, what your case is worth, and what happens if it goes to court. But none of that matters if the foundation isn't solid. Start here.

CHAPTER 1

WHAT TO DO WHEN YOU FALL

You didn't plan for this. One moment you were walking through a store, a parking lot, or a government office. The next moment you were on the ground.

Maybe you're reading this book because a fall already happened. Maybe you picked it up after you started dealing with medical bills, missed work, or an insurance company that won't return your calls. That's okay. This chapter explains what to do right after a fall—but it also helps you understand what matters most if your fall already happened.

Safety Comes First

Your health and safety matter more than any legal claim. If you've been hurt, focus on that first. Everything else is secondary.

If you're still near an active hazard—a slippery floor, a broken step, an unstable surface—move to safety if you can do so without making your injuries worse. If others might encounter the same hazard, warn them if you can do it safely.

If your injuries are serious, call 911 or ask someone to do so for you. That's the number for ambulance dispatch, not just police. If you can't move on your own, or if you're experiencing severe pain, dizziness, or any symptom that concerns you, get emergency medical help.

For less severe situations, get to an urgent care clinic, emergency room, or your primary care provider as soon as you can. If you have any sense at all that you've been injured, get checked out professionally.

Falls can be embarrassing. The natural impulse is to jump up, brush yourself off, and act like nothing happened. Fight that impulse. Injuries don't always announce themselves immediately. I've worked many cases where the injuries seemed minor at first but became much worse over the following days and weeks.

Getting checked out doesn't commit you to anything. It protects your health. And if you do end up pursuing a claim later, prompt medical attention creates a record that connects your injuries to the fall.

Document What Happened

Once the immediate crisis has passed and you're safe, start documenting. The evidence you gather in the first minutes and hours after a fall can make or break your case months down the road.

Take photographs. Almost everyone carries a smartphone these days. Use it. Photograph the hazard that caused your fall—the wet floor, the cracked sidewalk, the loose carpet, the broken step. Photograph the surrounding area. These don't need to be professional-quality images. Just do your best to capture what you see.

Why does this matter so much? Once a fall happens, property owners often fix the problem quickly. That's good for preventing future accidents. But it means the evidence of what caused your fall can disappear within hours. A photograph taken at the scene is the most powerful evidence you can have.

Get the location details. This sounds obvious, but people overlook it all the time. Get the exact address where you fell. Take pictures of the building exterior, the street address, the suite number if there is one. Photograph the street signs at the nearest intersection.

If you're inside a business, look for any business licenses displayed on the wall and photograph those. The company that operates a location is sometimes different from the name on the sign outside. Business licenses identify who actually runs the place.

Identify witnesses. Did anyone see you fall? Did anyone see the hazard before you fell? Get their full name and contact information—not just a first name. This includes people you were with, bystanders, and employees.

I've had many potential clients tell me that someone else saw exactly what happened. When I ask for that person's contact information, they give me a first name only—or nothing at all. Without a full name and a way to reach them, you don't have a witness. You have an allegation of a witness. That's not the same thing.

Report the Incident

If you fell at a business, commercial property, or any organization with management on site, report the incident before you leave.

Ask management to complete an incident report. Request that they follow whatever procedures they have in place for accidents. Most businesses have these protocols. Some are better than others.

Once the report is complete, ask for a copy. They may or may not give you one. Ask anyway.

Ask the organization to preserve any surveillance video that may have captured your fall. Many businesses have security cameras. Footage gets recorded over quickly—sometimes within days. A prompt request puts them on notice to save it.

What if they won't cooperate? Some managers will refuse to complete a report. Some will say "we don't do that here." If this happens, stay calm. Ask for the name of the person refusing. Ask to speak with a higher-level manager. Record whatever names and information you can gather.

Don't get into a confrontation. Be polite. Be firm. And document their refusal as part of your notes about what happened.

What if the report contains errors? If management completes a report but gets the facts wrong, ask for the opportunity to add your own written statement. You want the record to reflect what actually happened. Do your best to set it straight, but again—stay polite and professional.

Common Mistakes to Avoid

After working many slip, trip, and fall cases, I see the same mistakes again and again.

Assuming it's no big deal. New Mexicans pride themselves on being tough and self-reliant. There's an impulse to brush off a fall, to minimize it, to move on as quickly as possible. I understand that. But taking a few minutes to document what happened and getting checked by a doctor doesn't commit you to pursuing a claim. It just preserves your options.

You might never need those photographs or that incident report. But if your injuries turn out to be worse than you thought, you'll be very glad you have them.

Not getting witness contact information. A witness who saw the hazard or the fall can make a real difference in your case. But only if you can find them later. Full name. Phone number. Email if possible. Write it down before you leave the scene.

Failing to photograph the hazard. I can't stress this enough. Hazards get cleaned up. Broken things get fixed. That wet spot on the floor will be mopped within the hour. The photograph you take right after your fall may be the only evidence that the hazard ever existed.

When You Fall Alone

What if no one was with you? What if there were no witnesses?

Do the best you can. Take photographs if you're able. If your injuries prevent you from documenting the scene, return later—or ask a friend or family member to go back for you. Even photographs taken a day or two later are better than nothing, though they're most valuable when taken immediately.

When to Call 911

Call 911 if you need an ambulance. That's what emergency dispatch is for. If your injuries are severe enough that you can't move on your own, or if you need emergency medical transport, make that call.

What about police? For a typical slip, trip, or fall case, police involvement isn't needed or appropriate. These cases involve negligence—someone failed to maintain their property safely. That's a civil matter, not a criminal one.

Police involvement makes sense only if you believe a crime occurred. Did someone create the hazard intentionally? Did your fall result from a physical altercation? Those situations are rare, and they're mostly beyond the scope of this book. We focus on cases involving negligence—where someone failed to exercise ordinary care for the safety of others.

If You Didn't Know This Before Your Fall

You probably didn't have this book in your hands when you fell. Most people pick it up only after they're already dealing with a claim.

If you didn't take photographs, didn't get witness information, or didn't request an incident report—that's okay. You didn't know. Work with your attorney to address any gaps in documentation and figure out the best path forward with the evidence you do have.

The steps in this chapter give you the best foundation for a strong case. But cases succeed all the time even when the injured person didn't do everything perfectly at the scene. Don't assume your situation is hopeless just because you didn't know what to do in the moment.

Action Steps

After a fall on someone else's property:

1. **Get to safety** and address any immediate medical needs.
2. **Seek medical attention** if you have any sense you may be injured.

3. **Photograph everything**—the hazard, the scene, the address, any business licenses displayed.
4. **Get witness information**—full names and contact details.
5. **Report the incident** to management and request a copy of any report.
6. **Ask that surveillance footage be preserved.**
7. **Stay calm and professional**, even if you encounter resistance.
8. **Return later** if you couldn't gather information at the scene.

Your job right now is to protect your health and preserve your options. What comes next—whether to pursue a claim and how—is a decision you can make later, with better information and professional guidance.

CHAPTER 2

WHY PREMISES CASES ARE DIFFERENT

If you've ever known someone who was in a car accident and filed an injury claim, you might think you have a sense of how these things work. You get hurt. You deal with insurance. You get compensated.

It's not quite that simple. We offer another book, *New Mexico Car Accident Claims: A 505 Legal Guide*, that explains the nuts and bolts of motor vehicle collision injury claims.

But the fact is, slip, trip, and fall cases are generally more complicated and challenging than automobile collisions. They're often harder to prove, more expensive to pursue, and less intuitive for everyone involved—including the jurors who might eventually decide your case. Understanding these differences now will help you make better decisions and set realistic expectations as your case moves forward.

Liability Is Less Clear-Cut

In a car accident, fault often seems obvious. Someone ran a red light. Someone crossed the center line. Someone rear-ended another driver at a stoplight. The rules of the road are familiar to everyone, and violations are usually easy to identify.

Fall cases are different. The first question everyone asks—insurance adjusters, defense attorneys, and eventually jurors—is whether anyone was actually at fault at all.

Sometimes people fall and it's nobody's fault. Genuine accidents happen. A person trips on a perfectly normal sidewalk curb. Someone loses their balance for no particular reason. Not every fall means someone else did something wrong.

And even when a genuine hazard existed, the next question is whether you share some of the blame. Were you watching where you were going? Were you wearing appropriate footwear? Were you distracted by your phone? Should you have noticed the hazard and avoided it?

In car accident cases, these arguments come up occasionally. In fall cases, they come up almost every time. Insurance companies and defense attorneys will nearly always argue that the injured person is partly or fully responsible for what happened. And that argument has real traction with juries.

How Comparative Fault Works in New Mexico

New Mexico follows what's called a "comparative fault" rule. This means that if you're found partly responsible for your own injuries, your recovery is reduced in proportion to your share of the fault.

Here's how the math works. Say a jury determines that your total damages—medical bills, lost wages, pain and suffering—add up to $50,000. But they also find that you were 30% at fault for the accident, maybe because you weren't watching where you stepped.

You don't get $50,000. You get $35,000. Your recovery is reduced by your percentage of fault.

This calculation applies in every case where the injured person shares any responsibility. And in fall cases, defense attorneys push hard to put as much fault as possible on the person who fell. Even if there was a genuine hazard caused by negligence, they'll argue you should have seen it and stepped around it.

Context Changes Everything

Car accident cases follow relatively consistent rules. The rules of the road are the rules of the road. There are some differences—city driving versus highway driving, for example—but the basic framework stays the same.

Fall cases are far more context-dependent. What counts as a hazard, and what level of care a property owner must provide, changes drastically based on the situation.

A rough, uneven surface might be completely unacceptable on the polished floor of a shopping center. That same surface might be perfectly normal and expected on a trail at a state park.

A puddle of water a few feet from the showers in a gym locker room is one thing. People expect wet floors near showers. A puddle in the middle of a grocery store aisle is something else entirely.

Though it's not always spelled out in law, people—including jurors—tend to evaluate a small family-owned store differently than a national big-box retailer. They expect more from organizations with more resources.

If a facility specifically serves people with mobility limitations—a hospital, a nursing home, a rehabilitation center—the standards are different again. These organizations know their visitors may have difficulty navigating hazards that wouldn't trouble most people.

Restaurants present their own analysis. There's constant activity and a high risk of spills. What's reasonable to expect from a restaurant differs from what's reasonable to expect from an office building lobby.

Even the time of day matters. Your expectations are different when a business is open and staffed versus when it's closed and empty.

And New Mexico is a big state with dramatically different weather patterns. What counts as reasonable snow and ice removal in Taos or Red River—communities that deal with winter weather for months—is different from what's reasonable in Hobbs or Deming, where snow is less common.

Another factor we'll explore in detail later is whether the property owner had notice of the hazard. Did they know about it? Should they have known? How long had it existed before you encountered it? These questions matter enormously in premises cases.

The bottom line: each industry, each type of property, each human activity comes with its own set of expectations. The question is always what's normal, expected, and appropriate in this particular situation?

Jurors Don't Intuitively Understand Fall Injuries

Most people have an intuitive sense of the forces involved in a car accident. Two vehicles colliding at speed—it's easy to understand how that could cause serious injury. The violence of the event is obvious.

Falls are different. The question jurors often have, whether they say it out loud or not, is: how could someone be hurt that badly just from falling a few feet? I've fallen before. I wasn't injured like that.

The human body is complex. The severity of a fall injury depends on angles, on which body parts absorb the impact, on the surface you land on, on countless variables that aren't visible to someone who wasn't there. But explaining that to a jury takes work.

This challenge is especially acute when the injuries involve only soft tissue—muscles, ligaments, tendons—rather than broken bones. A fracture shows up on an X-ray. It's concrete. Soft tissue damage can cause years of pain and require extensive rehabilitation, but it's harder to see and harder to explain.

For jurors who have never experienced a serious fall injury, it can be difficult to understand how the effects could last so long or require so much treatment. This skepticism affects how they evaluate damages—and ultimately, how much they're willing to award.

Higher Costs to Pursue

Because liability is more complex in fall cases, they often cost more to pursue than car accident cases.

If someone runs a red light and causes a collision, you typically don't need to hire an expert to explain why that was negligent. The violation speaks for itself.

In a fall case, it can be different. How exactly was that gap in the sidewalk dangerous? Why should the property owner have known about that worn carpet? What industry standards apply to floor maintenance in a grocery store?

Answering these questions often requires a safety expert—someone who can explain to a jury why the condition was hazardous and why the property owner should have addressed it. That's an additional expert, with additional costs, beyond the medical experts you might need in any injury case.

These costs add up. They factor into the economics of your case and influence decisions about whether and how to pursue a claim.

The Insurance Difference

Not everything about premises cases is harder. One potential advantage: when a business or commercial property is at fault, they typically carry commercial insurance policies. These policies often have much higher coverage limits than the minimum auto insurance policies many drivers carry.

In car accident cases, it's common for the at-fault driver's insurance to be inadequate—their policy limits may be lower than the injured person's actual damages. In premises cases involving businesses, this is less often a problem.

Realistic Expectations

Clients sometimes come to me with expectations shaped by headlines about massive verdicts. It's important to understand what different case values actually reflect.

Cases that settle or result in verdicts in the hundreds of thousands of dollars typically involve very serious injuries—surgeries, lengthy hospital stays, years of treatment and rehabilitation.

Cases that reach into the millions involve catastrophic outcomes: paralysis, traumatic brain injury, death, permanent inability to perform the activities of daily living.

If you're able to work after your fall, you're going to need to continue working after your settlement. A premises liability claim compensates you for your losses. It doesn't transform your financial life.

These realities, combined with the liability challenges and costs we've discussed, all factor into what constitutes a reasonable settlement range for your particular case.

Good Results Are Within Reach

This chapter has painted a challenging picture. That's intentional. You need to understand what you're facing.

But here's the encouraging truth: good results are absolutely achievable in premises liability cases. It requires working with an attorney who knows these cases, understands their unique dynamics, and has a game plan for addressing the challenges.

These cases typically require more investigation and more litigation than a straightforward car accident. That's okay. You just need to connect with someone who can handle that level of work.

What matters most is that you and your attorney have a serious conversation about your specific situation. What are the challenges in your case? What do the damages look like? Where does the fault lie? Is an outcome that meets your goals reasonably likely?

The important thing is making sure the whole team—and that means both you and your attorney—shares a mutual understanding of the challenges, the risks, the possible outcomes, and the game plan for addressing them. When that communication and understanding exist, fair results are within reach.

Why This Book Exists

That's the purpose of this book. We want to give you, as the injured person, a foundation for partnering effectively with your attorney.

You don't need a law degree to participate meaningfully in your own case. But you do need to understand how these cases work, what makes them challenging, and what role you play in achieving a good outcome.

The chapters that follow will build that foundation—covering everything from finding the right attorney to understanding liability to navigating the settlement process. By the end, you'll be equipped to work alongside your legal team as an informed, effective partner.

That partnership is how premises cases succeed.

CHAPTER 3

WHO THIS BOOK IS FOR

Before we go further, let's make sure this book is right for your situation. It's designed for a specific type of case, and you should know upfront whether yours fits.

This Book Is For You If...

This book is for anyone who has been injured by a physical hazard in New Mexico and is wondering whether they need a lawyer, trying to find the right lawyer, or already working with a lawyer and wanting to make that relationship a success.

The most common situations involve slips, trips, and falls—stepping on a wet floor, tripping over broken pavement, falling on an icy sidewalk. But physical hazards take other forms too. Maybe you fell into an unmarked hole. Maybe a piece of a building—a loose ceiling tile, a broken fixture—fell and struck you. Maybe snow or ice slid off a roof and injured you.

What ties these situations together is that a physical condition of someone else's property caused your injury. The property owner, or whoever was responsible for maintaining it, failed to address a hazard. You were hurt as a result.

If that describes your situation, this book can help you understand how these cases work, what to expect, and how to work effectively with an attorney to pursue a fair outcome.

You Must Have Been Injured in New Mexico

This book covers New Mexico law. If your fall occurred in New Mexico, the information here applies to you—even if you live in another state.

But if you're a New Mexico resident and your fall happened somewhere else, this book isn't your guide. The rules of the state where you fell are what matter. A fall in Texas, Colorado, or Arizona means Texas, Colorado, or Arizona law applies, regardless of where you live.

What This Book Doesn't Cover

Some situations involve falls or injuries on property but fall outside what this book addresses.

Injuries from criminal acts or the conduct of other people. Cases involving shootings, assaults, sexual violence, or nursing home abuse and neglect are sometimes classified as "premises liability" in a legal sense. The theory is that the property owner failed to provide adequate security or supervision. But these cases involve very different facts, legal theories, and strategies than the slip, trip, and fall cases this book covers. The same goes for dog bites and animal attacks. If your injury resulted from another person's intentional or criminal conduct, or from an animal, you need guidance specific to that type of case.

Products liability cases. If you were injured on someone's property but the cause was a defective product—you were burned by a malfunctioning tanning bed, injured by faulty gym equipment, hurt by a collapsing chair—that's a products liability case, not a premises case. Different rules apply. This book won't help you navigate that.

Workers' compensation claims. If you were injured at your own workplace, or were otherwise hurt while on the job, workers' compensation is a separate legal system with its own rules and procedures. Even if your injury involved a slip, trip, or fall, the workers' comp system—not ordinary premises liability law—governs your situation.

There's one exception that can get complicated. Say you were working, but the injury happened on someone else's property due to their negligence—not your employer's. A delivery driver who slips on an icy walkway at a customer's location, for example. In that situation, you might have both a workers' compensation claim and a separate injury claim against the negligent property owner. This book might apply to the second claim, but the interaction between the two is complex. You need to discuss the specifics with an attorney.

Injuries on your own property. If you fell at your own home or on property you own, and you were solely responsible for the condition that caused your fall, there's typically no case. Premises liability is about holding property owners accountable for hazards they created or failed to fix. If you're the property owner, there's typically no one else to hold accountable. That said, if someone else created a hazard on your property, you may have a claim. Talk to your attorney if you believe you're in that situation.

Situations where you created the hazard. If you were personally responsible for the dangerous condition—say you knocked a jar of pickles off a grocery store shelf and then slipped on the spilled brine—you likely don't have a case. The property owner isn't responsible for a hazard you created moments before your fall. That said, the details matter. If you're unsure whether this applies to your situation, discuss it with an attorney.

When You're Not Sure

If you've read through these categories and you're still uncertain whether this book applies to your situation, the best step is to consult with an attorney. Many offer free initial consultations for injury cases. A lawyer can quickly assess whether your situation fits within ordinary premises liability law or falls into a different category that requires different expertise.

Don't assume you don't have a case just because your situation seems complicated or doesn't fit neatly into one box. And don't assume you do have a case just because you were hurt on someone else's property. Get professional guidance to know for sure.

If your situation does fit what this book covers—an injury caused by a physical hazard on someone else's property in New Mexico—then read on. The chapters ahead will give you the foundation you need to navigate the process and work effectively with your legal team.

CHAPTER 4

DO YOU NEED A LAWYER?

You're walking down the aisle at a big-box home improvement store. You're thinking about your project, scanning the shelves. Then, without warning, your feet fly out from under you. You land hard on your tailbone. Pain shoots through your lower back.

As you wince and try to process what just happened, you feel something wet on your hands. It's paint. There's a can on its side a few feet away, and wet paint has formed a puddle across the floor. That's what you slipped in.

A store employee rushes over. A manager appears. They help you up, complete an incident report, and express concern. They give you some paper towels. Maybe they offer to call an ambulance.

Now what?

The Misconception

Most people believe insurance companies make things right after an accident. You can't blame them. Watch any insurance commercial and you'll see friendly agents, reassuring slogans, and lots of promises. The message is clear: when something goes wrong, we're here to help.

Here's what those commercials don't tell you. The store's insurance company has no duty to you. Their duty runs to their client—the business that pays their premiums. Their job is to protect the insured, typically by resolving your claim for as little money as possible.

Let that sink in. The company you're about to deal with has a financial incentive to pay you less.

The Early Offer Trap

A few days after the fall, an adjuster calls. They're polite. They express concern about your injuries. Then they make an offer. Maybe $2,500. Maybe $5,000.

If you've only been to urgent care, that number might look reasonable. You're sore, you missed some work, you have a few hundred dollars in medical bills. A few thousand dollars would help right now.

But here's what you don't know yet. Six months from now, you might still be in physical therapy. Your back might require injections or even surgery. Your eventual medical bills might exceed that early offer.

To get any money from the insurance company, you'll need to sign a release. That release is final. It covers everything—past, present, and future claims arising from your fall. Once you sign, you cannot go back for more. Ever.

The insurance company knows this. That's why they call early.

The Phone Call You Didn't Expect

Let's say you don't take the early offer. You call the adjuster to explain what happened, expecting a straightforward conversation. You're the victim here. There was paint on the floor. You fell. You got hurt. Simple.

Instead, the questions start.

What shoes were you wearing? Were they flat or heeled? What kind of soles? Were you actually shopping, or were you just walking through? Did you make a purchase that day? After you fell, did you continue shopping? How long did you stay in the store?

Did you see the paint before you stepped in it? Was there a wet floor sign nearby? Were you looking at your phone? Were you distracted by something?

How old are you? Do you have any balance issues? Have you fallen before? Do you have any mobility limitations? Any prior back injuries?

Suddenly you feel like a suspect. You came into this call as the victim. Now you're defending yourself.

This isn't an accident. The adjuster is doing their job.

Why All Those Questions Matter

As we discussed in Chapter 2, New Mexico is a comparative negligence state. If you share any fault for the accident—even a little—your recovery gets reduced proportionally.

Here's the math again. Say your case is worth $40,000. The store clearly should have cleaned up the paint spill. But the insurance company argues you should have been watching where you walked. A jury finds you 25% responsible.

Now your $40,000 case is worth $30,000.

That's why adjusters ask about your shoes. About your phone. About whether you saw the hazard. About whether you kept shopping afterward. They're looking for anything that shifts fault onto you or minimizes your injuries.

The question about continuing to shop is particularly telling. If you stayed in the store for another hour after your fall, they'll argue your injuries couldn't have been that serious. You're building their defense for them.

They're also probing for reasons you might be prone to falling regardless of the paint. Prior falls. Balance issues. Age-related concerns. Anything that suggests this fall wasn't really the store's fault—or that your injuries stem from pre-existing conditions rather than this incident.

And they're watching for signs of fraud. Staged falls are a real concern for retailers. Questions about whether you were actually shopping, whether you made a purchase, and the details of how the fall happened are partly designed to sniff out claims that don't add up.

Every answer you give is being used to build a case—against you.

When People Realize They Need Help

Some people figure this out after a few frustrating phone calls. The process isn't what they expected. They're not getting answers. They feel like they're fighting rather than being helped.

Others realize it when they see the release the insurance company wants them to sign. Legal language. Finality. The weight of what they're being asked to give up becomes real.

Some people realize it when they understand what they're actually up against. Insurance companies have spent decades building systems—algorithms, databases, automated processes—designed to resolve claims quickly and cheaply. The adjuster you're negotiating with may have limited authority to deviate from what those systems recommend. You're not just negotiating with a person. You're pushing against a machine.

And in premises cases, as Chapter 2 explained, you're also pushing against skepticism that's baked into how people view falls. Jurors who've never experienced a serious fall injury may not understand how one fall could lead to months of treatment. The insurance company knows this and factors it into their offers.

More and more people are figuring it out before they even talk to the insurance company. They understand that professional help usually leads to better results.

There's no wrong time to call an attorney. But earlier is usually better than later—especially before you've signed anything or given a recorded statement.

One more reason timing matters: deadlines. In New Mexico, most injury claims must be filed within three years. That sounds like a long time—until months slip by while you're focused on recovery, and suddenly it isn't.

Three years is the general rule, but important variations exist. If your fall occurred on government property—a city sidewalk, a state building, a public school—the New Mexico Tort Claims Act imposes much shorter notice requirements. Miss those deadlines and your claim may be barred entirely, no matter how strong it is.

This is an area where you don't want to take chances.

What a Lawyer Actually Does

You might think hiring a lawyer just means having someone negotiate on your behalf. That's part of it. But an experienced premises liability attorney does much more, even before your case gets anywhere near a courtroom.

Managing critical deadlines. Your attorney identifies, calendars, and tracks deadlines that could kill your claim—the statute of limitations, Tort Claims Act notice requirements for government property cases, and other time-sensitive obligations. These aren't just important. They're absolute. Miss them and your case is over.

Tracing all involved entities. This is detective work, and it's essential. The company whose name is on the building may not own the property. The landowner may lease to a tenant. The tenant may contract out maintenance to a third party. If you fell on a sidewalk, the municipality may share responsibility. Your attorney digs through property records, lease agreements, and corporate structures to identify everyone who might be liable. Miss a responsible party and you might miss the coverage that would pay your claim.

Sending preservation letters. Once responsible parties are identified, your attorney sends formal notice that a claim exists and that evidence must be preserved. This includes surveillance footage, incident reports, maintenance logs, and anything else relevant to your case. These letters matter. If a company destroys evidence after receiving proper notice, they can face serious sanctions.

Gathering evidence. Incident reports from the property owner. Surveillance footage. Maintenance records. Prior complaints about similar hazards. If your fall occurred on government property, public records requests. An attorney knows what to ask for and how to get it.

Gathering your medical records and bills. This sounds simple. It isn't. Medical providers use different systems. Physicians bill separately from hospitals. Bills arrive months after treatment. Physical therapy records come from somewhere else entirely. An attorney's office has processes for tracking all of it down.

Handling subrogation. If your health insurance paid for accident-related treatment, they may have a right to be repaid from your settlement. This is called subrogation. Miss this step and you could face serious problems later—including demands for repayment after you've already spent the money.

Medicare compliance. If you're a Medicare recipient, complex rules govern how your settlement interacts with the program. These rules carry legal penalties for noncompliance. Your attorney ensures everything is handled properly.

Coordinating with expert witnesses. As we discussed in Chapter 2, premises cases often require experts that car accident cases don't. A safety expert may need to explain why the condition was hazardous and what standards the property owner violated. Medical experts may need to explain how a fall caused your injuries. Your attorney identifies, retains, and coordinates with these witnesses.

Building a professional demand package. This is the document that presents your case to the insurance company. It pulls together the evidence, the medical records, the bills, and the legal arguments. It looks different from a letter you'd write yourself.

Valuing your claim. What is your case actually worth? An attorney who handles premises cases regularly knows how similar injuries have settled. They know what juries in New Mexico have awarded.

They can calibrate a demand that reflects reality—accounting for the liability challenges that are common in fall cases.

The signaling effect. Insurance companies track attorneys. They know who files lawsuits. They know who takes cases to trial. They know who settles everything. When an attorney with a reputation for trying cases sends a demand letter, it changes how the insurance company evaluates the claim.

Taking the case to litigation if necessary. If the insurance company won't offer a fair settlement, your attorney can file suit and take the case to court. That means filings, discovery, depositions, motions, and potentially trial. It's a different level of work entirely—and it's leverage you don't have on your own.

Insurance in Premises Cases

One difference from car accident cases: insurance is typically simpler on your side. You're usually not dealing with your own auto insurance, UM/UIM coverage, or multiple policies on your vehicles.

Instead, it comes down to what coverage the at-fault parties have. A typical commercial general liability policy provides $1 million in coverage. Some businesses carry excess policies on top of that. And if multiple parties are responsible—the landlord, the tenant, a maintenance company—each may have its own insurance.

The good news is that commercial policies usually have higher limits than the minimum auto insurance many drivers carry. The challenge is identifying all the responsible parties and their coverage, which is part of the detective work your attorney performs.

When You Don't Need a Lawyer

Not every fall requires an attorney. If your claim is small enough that attorney fees would eat up most of the recovery, it may not make economic sense.

Attorneys typically work on contingency in personal injury cases, meaning they take a percentage of what you recover. For small claims, that math doesn't always work for either side.

If you weren't really injured—just embarrassed or inconvenienced—there may not be a case worth pursuing at all.

Here's something important to understand: injury cases are built on the severity of injuries. That's what drives the value of a claim. If your biggest concern is that you felt disrespected after the incident—the manager was rude, the staff didn't take you seriously, nobody apologized, the company never followed up—that's frustrating, but it's not something a lawyer can help with.

I understand why people feel this way. You fell on someone else's property because of their negligence. The least they could do is treat you with dignity and concern. When that doesn't happen, it adds insult to injury.

But the legal system compensates for injuries, not for poor customer service or hurt feelings. If your physical injuries are minor but you're upset about how you were treated, pursuing a legal claim probably isn't the answer. No attorney can get you the apology or acknowledgment you deserve. What we can do is pursue fair compensation for real injuries—and that requires real injuries to pursue.

The Bottom Line

Here's what I tell people who aren't sure they need a lawyer: if you're not convinced I'm adding value, it's probably not a good fit. I'm not selling used cars. There's plenty of work out there. If you think you can do just as well on your own, go for it.

But I encourage you to read through this book first.

Think about whether you have the time to trace every potentially responsible party through property records. Think about whether you know the notice deadlines for government property cases. Think about whether you can identify the experts your case might need. Think about whether you understand subrogation rules and Medicare compliance.

Think about whether you're ready for the questions the adjuster will ask—and whether you know how your answers will be used.

Then decide.

CHAPTER 5

FINDING THE RIGHT ATTORNEY

You've decided you need a lawyer. Now what?

Finding the right attorney matters. This could be a relationship that lasts years. The person you choose will handle a significant financial matter on your behalf. You need someone you trust, someone who communicates clearly, and someone who knows what they're doing.

Here's how to find that person.

Start with People You Trust

The best way to find an attorney is through someone who has actually worked with one. Not someone who saw a billboard. Not someone who heard a name somewhere. Someone who hired an attorney, went through a case, and can tell you what the experience was really like.

Ask around. A friend, family member, or coworker who has been through an injury claim can tell you things no advertisement ever will. Did the attorney return calls? Did they explain things clearly?

Did the client feel respected throughout the process? Did they get a result they felt good about?

If someone you trust had a good experience with an attorney, that's worth more than any marketing budget.

What Ads Can and Can't Tell You

Most people start their search with advertising. Google results, television commercials, billboards along the interstate. That's natural. You go with what's familiar.

There's nothing wrong with using ads as a starting point. But understand what they are: marketing. An ad tells you that an attorney or firm spent money to reach you. It doesn't tell you whether they'll do a good job on your case.

The only way to know if an attorney is right for you is to ask questions.

What Actually Separates Good from Mediocre

Three things matter most when evaluating a premises liability attorney.

Do they listen? Any good attorney begins with a genuine effort to understand your situation. Not just the facts of your fall, but your goals. What matters to you? What are you worried about? What outcome would make this feel resolved? An attorney who jumps to conclusions without listening isn't someone you want handling your case.

Do they handle premises cases routinely? A general practice attorney can handle a basic injury claim. But as we discussed in Chapter 2, premises cases are a different ballgame from car accidents. The liability questions are more complex. The defense arguments are more aggressive. The expert witness needs are different.

An attorney who handles premises liability cases regularly will spot issues that a generalist might miss. They'll know how defense attorneys approach these cases. They'll understand the unique challenges of proving fault when the other side is arguing you should have watched where you were going.

Ask specifically about their premises liability experience. How many slip, trip, and fall cases have they handled? What were the outcomes? Don't assume that experience with car accidents translates directly.

Can they handle the complexity? This is the real differentiator in premises cases. As we covered in Chapter 4, these cases require detective work that goes beyond a typical injury claim.

Can this attorney trace all the potentially responsible parties—the landowner, the building owner, the tenant, the maintenance contractor, the municipality? Do they know how to dig through property records and corporate structures to find everyone who might be liable?

Do they have relationships with safety experts? In many premises cases, you'll need an expert to explain why the condition was hazardous and what standards the property owner violated. An attorney who handles these cases regularly will have experts they've worked with before—professionals they trust to explain complex issues clearly to a jury.

An attorney who only understands basic liability—who did what to whom—may not be equipped to navigate the layers of responsibility that premises cases often involve.

Why the Numbers Don't Mean Much

You'll see firms advertise case volume, average settlements, or headline verdicts. These numbers feel meaningful. They're not.

Think about it. As the number of cases a firm handles goes up, the average settlement almost has to go down. More cases means more smaller cases in the mix. A high volume of cases at lower values doesn't indicate skill. It might just reflect the population the firm serves.

What about million-dollar verdicts? Those happen when injuries are catastrophic and insurance coverage is substantial. An attorney who won a million-dollar verdict can't replicate that result on your case unless your injuries and coverage justify it. What somebody else got doesn't tell you what your case is worth.

Settlement values depend on factors the attorney doesn't control: how badly you were hurt, how much insurance is available, how clear the liability is. In premises cases, liability is often contested—which makes advertised numbers even less meaningful.

Get away from the numbers. Get back to the relationship.

Ask yourself: Has this person taken the time to explain things clearly? Do I feel like they understand my situation? Can I see myself working with them for potentially years?

Questions to Ask

When you meet with an attorney, come prepared. These questions will help you evaluate whether this person is the right fit.

- What's your specific experience with slip, trip, and fall cases?

- How will you identify all potentially responsible parties in my case?
- Do you have particular safety experts you like to work with? Why do you like them?
- How will we know when it's time to settle?
- Are your fees different if we file a lawsuit? If we go to trial?
- Will I receive a cost breakdown before settling?
- How do you advise clients who aren't sure whether a settlement offer is appropriate?
- Walk me through the claims negotiation process.
- Walk me through what litigation looks like if we can't settle.
- How will you investigate my case?

Pay attention to how the attorney answers, not just what they say. Are they patient? Are they clear? Do they treat you like a partner in this process, or like someone to be managed?

An attorney's willingness to explain things thoroughly tells you a lot about how they'll treat you throughout your case.

Red Flags

Some things should make you walk away.

High-pressure sales techniques. If an attorney tells you that you need to sign up right now, that's a red flag. A legitimate attorney doesn't need to pressure you into a decision.

Confusing fee arrangements. Fee structures should be clear and straightforward.

Guarantees or promises of results. No attorney can guarantee an outcome. They don't control enough variables. Anyone who promises you a specific result is either lying or doesn't understand their own profession. This is especially true in premises cases, where liability is frequently contested.

Minimizing legitimate questions. If you ask a reasonable question and the attorney brushes it off, that's a problem. Your questions matter. An attorney who doesn't respect them now won't respect them later.

Claims of special insider status. Be skeptical of attorneys who suggest they have special relationships with adjusters or judges. That's not how this works.

Sign-up bonuses. If an attorney offers you money just to sign with them, walk away. This is exploitative, unethical, and possibly illegal.

Unsolicited contact. If an attorney contacted you after your accident without you reaching out first, that's a serious red flag. Ethical attorneys don't chase ambulances.

Yellow Flags

Some things aren't necessarily problems, but they might mean this isn't the right fit.

Maybe the attorney seemed rushed or inattentive. Maybe their explanations didn't quite make sense to you. Maybe they lacked confidence or clarity when you asked about premises cases specifically. Maybe you just felt like you were on different wavelengths.

None of these are deal-breakers on their own. But this relationship could last years. Fit matters. If something feels off, trust that instinct and keep looking.

What a "Consultation" Actually Is

The legal industry uses the word "consultation" in a way that creates mismatched expectations.

For you, "consultation" might suggest you'll get actionable legal analysis of your situation, whether or not you hire the attorney. That's not what happens. It's more like asking a doctor whether you need surgery before they've looked at your x-rays. Without investigation, no responsible attorney can tell you what your case is worth or how it will turn out.

For the attorney, a consultation is an opportunity to learn about your case and decide whether it makes sense to take it. They'll ask questions about your fall, your injuries, where it happened, and what you know about the property owner. They'll give you general information about the process. But they won't—and shouldn't—give you specific legal advice before they've done their homework.

In New Mexico, consultations for personal injury cases are typically free. This is especially true for cases that will be handled on contingency. Expect the initial meeting to last fifteen to thirty minutes. That's usually enough time for an attorney to determine whether they can help.

Should you meet with multiple attorneys? Here's a simple test. After that first meeting, ask yourself: Did I feel treated with respect? Will I be comfortable entrusting this person with a significant financial matter? Can I see myself working with them for potentially years?

If you can answer yes, sign with that attorney. If you have doubts, keep looking.

New Mexico's Legal Landscape

Here's a reality about New Mexico: most cities and towns are small. Many have few attorneys. Some have none.

That creates a challenge. The traditional solo practitioner in a small community is often a generalist—handling injury claims alongside divorces, criminal defense, wills, and real estate. They may be perfectly competent, but they may not have deep experience with the complexities that can make or break a premises case.

The old trade-off used to be: local generalist or distant specialist. Pick one.

That's changing. Some firms, like 505 Legal, are dedicated to delivering accessibility without sacrificing expertise—using modern technology, responsive communication, and client-focused systems to serve communities across the state. A team-based approach, where attorneys concentrate on specific practice areas rather than spreading thin across everything, means you're not giving up depth to get service.

What matters isn't whether your attorney's office is down the street. What matters is whether you can reach them when you need to, whether they have real experience in New Mexico courtrooms, and whether they know New Mexico premises liability law—not just general principles, but the specific rules and practices that apply here.

Look for a firm that's accessible and responsive, with dedicated experience in New Mexico premises liability cases—not a solo generalist juggling too many practice areas, and not a distant billboard firm that treats you like a file number.

A Note on the Big Advertisers

You'll recognize some names from billboards and television. Some of those firms are excellent. Some are not. The advertising budget tells you nothing.

Ask questions. Is this a New Mexico firm, or an out-of-state operation looking at New Mexico as their next market? What's the firm's real presence in the state? Where are the attorneys from? Who will actually be working on your case? Is that person experienced in New Mexico courtrooms?

The name on the billboard might not be the person handling your file. Find out who will be.

The Right Fit

Finding an attorney isn't just about credentials and experience. It's about finding someone you can work with through what might be a long and sometimes frustrating process.

The right attorney will listen to you. They'll explain things clearly. They'll have real experience with premises cases and understand what makes them different. They'll treat you like a partner, not a file number.

Take the time to find that person. It matters.

CHAPTER 6

UNDERSTANDING FEE AGREEMENTS

Before you sign anything, you need to understand how you're going to pay your attorney. Fee agreements in personal injury cases work differently than in other areas of law. The structure can work in your favor—but only if you understand what you're agreeing to.

This chapter explains how fees work, what to watch for, and how to avoid surprises when your case resolves.

How Contingency Fees Work

Most personal injury claims in New Mexico are handled on a contingency fee basis. This means the attorney's fee is calculated as a percentage of your total recovery. If you don't recover anything, you don't pay a fee.

That's the basis for all those ads you've seen: "No fee unless we win."

In New Mexico, contingency fees for injury claims typically range from one-third (33⅓%) to 40% of the total recovery. That percentage typically applies to the gross amount received from the insurance company—before deduction of costs, before payment of outstanding medical bills or subrogation claims, before anything else comes out.

One additional detail: attorneys in New Mexico must pay gross receipts tax on their fees, and this is usually added to the amount you pay. GRT rates vary across the state depending on what state and local governments have imposed in different cities and counties. The rate that applies to your case is typically based on where your attorney's office is located. Expect somewhere between 5% and 9% of the fee amount to be added for GRT.

So if your fee is 40% and the GRT rate is 8%, the total for attorney compensation would be 40% plus 3.2% (which is 8% of 40%), for a combined 43.2% of the recovery.

The Difference Between Fees and Costs

People often confuse fees and costs. They're different, and understanding the distinction matters.

Fees are what the attorney is paid for their time and expertise. Think of it like labor in auto repair or construction. Under a contingency agreement, if there's no recovery, the attorney fee is zero.

Costs are payments made to others to move your case forward. These include copying charges for medical records, filing fees in the court system, payments to court reporters who transcribe depositions, and fees for expert witnesses. Think of costs like parts or materials in the construction analogy.

Legal cases typically involve much higher labor (fees) than materials (costs). But costs can still add up, especially in complex cases or cases that go to trial.

In premises liability cases, expert witness fees are often a significant cost component. As we discussed in earlier chapters, these cases frequently require safety experts to explain why a condition was hazardous and what standards the property owner violated. Unlike car accident cases where running a red light speaks for itself, a fall case may need an expert to establish that a gap in the sidewalk or a slippery floor coating fell below industry standards. These experts don't work for free, and their fees come out of the recovery as costs.

In many contingency fee agreements, the attorney or firm will advance costs as they arise and then get reimbursed from the recovery at the end of the case. Fees are usually calculated before reimbursement of these costs.

One important note: some clients assume that if there's no recovery, the attorney will absorb the costs. This is generally not permitted under the rules of professional conduct. Paying a client's costs is considered prohibited financial assistance in connection with a pending matter. In most fee agreements, you remain obligated for costs even if the case doesn't result in a recovery. Make sure you understand this before you sign.

Why Fee Percentages Vary

You might wonder why one attorney charges 33⅓% while another charges 40%. Is the more expensive attorney better? Is the cheaper one cutting corners?

Usually, neither. The difference in fee percentages typically has nothing to do with the complexity of your case or the quality of the attorney. It's simply about how that attorney or firm has chosen to position themselves in the market. Most firms have a standard fee structure they apply to all contingency matters they handle.

A higher fee doesn't necessarily mean better representation. A lower fee doesn't necessarily mean worse. Focus on the attorney's qualifications, communication style, and experience—not on saving a few percentage points.

Escalating Fee Structures

Some fee agreements start at one percentage and increase if certain things happen. For example, the fee might be one-third before litigation but increase to 40% if a lawsuit is filed. Other triggers might include going to trial or filing an appeal.

Some reputable and ethical attorneys use this structure. The justification is that certain stages of a case—filing suit, going to trial—require significantly more of the attorney's time. That's fair as far as it goes.

But I'm not a fan of escalating fees. The problem is that strategic decisions on your claim can become influenced by the attorney's fee rates. If filing a lawsuit bumps the fee from 33% to 40%, is the attorney's recommendation to file suit driven by what's best for your case or by what's best for their bottom line?

This concern is particularly relevant in premises cases. As we've discussed, these cases often require litigation to achieve a fair result. Insurance companies know that liability is harder to prove in fall cases, and they may offer less at the negotiation stage. If your attorney's fee increases when they file suit, you want to be confident that their recommendation to litigate—or not to litigate—is based on what's best for you.

This doesn't mean every attorney with an escalating fee structure is acting in bad faith. But it's a potential conflict you should be aware of. If you're considering an attorney with this structure, ask them directly how they handle the potential conflict. Their answer will tell you something.

Red Flags in Fee Arrangements

Most injury claims should be handled on contingency. If an attorney wants a deposit upfront or wants to charge you an hourly rate for a premises liability case, be skeptical. The attorney may believe you don't have a viable case and just wants to bill you for their time regardless of the outcome.

On the other end of the spectrum, if an attorney offers you money or some other financial assistance to sign up with them, that's a serious red flag. This is prohibited by the rules of professional conduct. Walk away.

What to Look for Before You Sign

Before signing a fee agreement, make sure you understand these key points.

What happens if you fire the attorney? Even on contingency matters, if you discharge the attorney before the case resolves, you could owe them something—often calculated based on their time at an hourly rate. This is fair. Under a contingency arrangement, attorneys only get paid if there's a successful outcome. If you fire them before they have the chance to land the plane, they're entitled to compensation for the work they've done.

Who pays costs, and when? Know whether the attorney will advance case costs or whether they have the right to require trust deposits from you. It's reasonable for an agreement to include a provision allowing the attorney to stop advancing costs and require you to pay them directly. The attorney is not a bank. They shouldn't be required to bankroll a client's decision to run up costs when the prospects of recovery don't justify it—say, if you insist on going to trial despite receiving a fair settlement offer.

This is worth understanding clearly in premises cases because costs can be higher than in simpler injury claims. If your case needs a safety expert, that's an expense. If it goes to litigation and requires depositions, those are expenses too. Make sure you understand how these will be handled.

When can the attorney withdraw? Understand the circumstances under which the attorney can withdraw from your case and what happens to fees and costs if they do.

All of these provisions are permitted under the rules of professional conduct and are ethical. But you need to be aware of them before you sign, not after.

Common Surprises at Settlement Time

When your case settles and the check arrives, you might be surprised by what comes out of it.

Medical liens and subrogation. If your health insurance paid for accident-related treatment, they may have a right to be repaid from your settlement. If Medicare or Medicaid was involved, there are other rules. We'll cover this in detail later in the book, but know that your recovery may be reduced by these obligations.

Case costs. If your case required depositions, expert witnesses, or extensive record gathering, the costs can add up. In premises cases that go to litigation, it's not unusual for costs to reach tens of thousands of dollars. This shouldn't be a complete surprise—there should be discussion along the way about what's happening and how much it costs. But clients sometimes underestimate how much these expenses total.

If You Already Have a Settlement Offer

Sometimes people come to an attorney after they've already received a settlement offer from the insurance company. If that's your situation, clarify one thing upfront: will the fee be calculated on the total settlement at the end, or just on the increase the attorney achieves for you?

Which approach is appropriate depends on the size of the offer you already have. If you come in with a typical lowball, pre-litigation offer—say, $3,000—an attorney would reasonably expect to calculate their fee on the total recovery. But if you come in with a substantial offer already on the table, the calculation might be different.

The key principle: you should not end up worse off for having hired counsel. A good attorney will structure the fee to make sure that's the case. Ask about this directly before signing.

Will the Other Side Pay My Attorney's Fees?

Clients sometimes ask whether the insurance company will be required to pay their attorney's fees on top of the settlement—as an add-on rather than something that comes out of their recovery.

In almost all cases, the answer is no. The insurance company will offer a single sum to resolve the case. They may factor potential attorney involvement into that number, but it's not broken out separately. The fee comes from your recovery.

In some cases, where there's an additional legal claim beyond typical negligence—certain statutory claims, for example—there may be grounds to seek an award of attorney's fees from the other side. If this possibility exists in your case, the fee agreement should address how that figures into the fee calculation.

The Bottom Line

Fee agreements aren't complicated, but they do require attention. Before you sign, make sure you understand the percentage, the difference between fees and costs, what happens if the relationship ends early, and how costs will be handled—especially the expert witness costs that premises cases often require.

A good attorney will take the time to explain all of this clearly. If you have questions, ask them before you sign. The answers matter.

CHAPTER 7

WHAT TO EXPECT FROM YOUR LAWYER (AND WHAT THEY EXPECT FROM YOU)

You've hired an attorney. Now what?

A personal injury case is a working relationship. It might last months. It might last years. Both sides have responsibilities. When expectations are clear from the start, everything goes smoother. When they're not, frustration builds on both sides.

This chapter explains what you should expect from your attorney, what your attorney expects from you, and how to keep the relationship on track.

The First Few Weeks

After you sign a fee agreement, the attorney's office gets to work gathering information. This phase is about building the file with everything needed to move your case forward.

On the incident itself, the firm needs whatever evidence you have—photographs of the hazard and the scene, the incident report if you obtained one, witness names and contact information. They'll also begin the work of identifying all potentially responsible parties: the property owner, the building owner if different, the tenant, any maintenance contractors, and the municipality if applicable. This detective work, which we discussed in Chapter 4, starts early.

On the medical side, they need to understand your current treatment status. What providers have you seen? What clinics? Are you still treating or are you finished? They'll also need your health insurance information, including whether you have Medicare or Medicaid. This matters for coordinating subrogation, liens, and compliance with rules around Medicare conditional payments.

On insurance, they need information about any coverage you're aware of. If a claim has already been opened with the property owner's insurance, they'll need the claim number.

Your attorney must also identify critical deadlines. Most importantly, there's the statute of limitations—miss it and your claim is gone, no matter how strong the case. But in premises cases, there may be other deadlines too. If your fall occurred on government property—a city sidewalk, a state building, a public facility—the New Mexico Tort Claims Act imposes notice requirements that are much shorter than the general statute of limitations. These deadlines are absolute. You shouldn't have to worry about tracking them yourself, but you should confirm your attorney has them calendared and is working with them in mind.

The first few weeks are all about populating the file with this basic information. From there, what happens next depends on where you are in your treatment.

If you're still treating, the case is likely in a holding pattern. The attorney can't make a demand until they know the full extent of your treatment. If you appear to be done treating, the firm may move toward preparing a demand or even filing litigation.

How Often Will You Hear from Your Attorney?

Communication depends on the stage of your case.

During treatment, don't expect frequent contact. If you're still seeing doctors and going to physical therapy, your attorney likely can't push the claim forward yet. You might hear from the firm every ninety days or so, just to check in and confirm your status. At this stage, communication is more about you keeping the attorney updated as your treatment progresses.

During litigation, communication should be more frequent. Unfortunately, many attorneys don't update clients as often as they should. Some only reach out when something notable happens. Look for a firm that has systems in place for routine updates so you're not left wondering what's going on with your own case.

One practical note: law firms are busy places. You should expect that some—or even most—of your conversations will be with staff members like paralegals or case managers rather than with the attorney directly. That's normal and doesn't mean your case isn't being handled properly.

But for any decision that needs to be made, the attorney should be involved. When it's time to evaluate a settlement offer, decide whether to file suit, or make any significant strategic choice, the attorney should be guiding you through it with adequate time and adequate explanation. If that's not happening, there's a problem.

What Your Attorney Expects from You

Your attorney needs you to do a few basic things.

Keep the firm updated on changes. If you move, change your phone number, get new health insurance, switch doctors, or start seeing a new provider, let your attorney's office know. Changes in your situation affect your case.

Respond when they contact you. If the firm reaches out and asks for something, it's because they need it to move your case forward. A request for a document, a signature, or a piece of information isn't busywork. Respond promptly.

Answer questions honestly and completely. Your attorney can only help you if they have accurate information. Don't leave things out because you think they might be embarrassing or unhelpful. Let your attorney decide what matters.

This isn't complicated. Stay in touch, respond to requests, and be honest. That's what makes someone a good client to work with.

The One Thing That Can Sink Your Case

Here's the most important thing I can tell you about your responsibilities as a client: don't lie.

Don't lie to your attorney. Don't lie to the insurance adjuster. Don't lie in a deposition. Don't lie anywhere.

I can work with almost anything except a lie. If you made a mistake, tell me. If something embarrassing happened, tell me. If there's a fact that seems bad for your case, tell me. I need to know so I can deal with it. Surprises from the other side are far worse than uncomfortable truths shared early.

This is especially important in premises cases. Remember, the defense will almost always argue that you share some fault for your fall. They'll dig into what you were doing, what you were wearing, whether you should have seen the hazard. If there's something that looks bad—you were distracted, you'd had a drink, you weren't wearing appropriate shoes—I need to know about it upfront. I can work with difficult facts if I know about them early. I can't recover from a lie exposed at a deposition.

What about social media? I'd prefer you don't talk about your case or post about it online. But as long as what you're posting is truthful, it's not an insurmountable problem. The real issue isn't social media—it's honesty.

If you tell the insurance company your injuries keep you bedridden, and then you post a video of yourself hiking, you have a problem. But that's a lying problem, not a social media problem. The platform just made the lie visible.

Tell the truth. Always. At certain times, your attorney might advise you not to volunteer information, but whenever you do speak on a topic, it needs to be the truth.

When Relationships Break Down

Attorney-client relationships fail for predictable reasons.

Lack of communication. Either the attorney isn't keeping the client informed, or the client isn't responding to the attorney's requests. Both cause problems.

Misaligned expectations. The client expected the case to move faster, or settle for more than reality allows.

Lack of action by the attorney. The case sits without progress. Deadlines get missed. Nothing seems to be happening.

Clients withholding or misrepresenting information. The attorney discovers facts that should have been disclosed earlier. Trust breaks down.

Not understanding timelines. Injury cases take time. Clients who expect quick resolutions get frustrated when the process stretches on.

Most of these problems can be prevented with clear communication from the start. That's why this chapter exists.

If You're Unhappy with Your Attorney

If you feel like your attorney isn't doing their job, the first step is simple: contact them and explain your concerns.

There may be good reasons for what looks like inaction. Your attorney might be working hard behind the scenes, waiting on something outside their control, or failing to communicate progress adequately. A conversation might resolve everything.

If you reach out and don't get a response, that's a different situation. If you get a response but the explanation doesn't make sense, that's also a problem.

You have the right to know what's happening with your case. If your attorney can't or won't explain, you may need to consider whether this is the right fit.

A word of caution before you make that decision: review your fee agreement. Depending on the contract you signed, you may owe your current attorney for time spent, costs advanced, or a portion of any eventual recovery—even if you switch to someone else. Discharging your attorney is your right, but it's not always free. Understand the financial implications before you act.

A Word on Case Value Expectations

Some clients come in with unrealistic ideas about what their case is worth. Maybe a friend got a big settlement. Maybe they saw a headline about a massive verdict. Maybe they just assume injuries mean a large payout.

As we discussed in Chapter 2, premises cases come with particular challenges. Liability is often contested. Juries don't intuitively understand fall injuries the way they understand car accidents. Defense attorneys almost always argue comparative fault. These realities affect case values.

If you think your attorney is undervaluing your case, ask questions. Ask for examples of similar cases. Ask about prior settlements for comparable injuries. Then evaluate what you hear reasonably.

Although every case is different, your case is probably not as unique as you think. Attorneys who handle premises liability claims regularly have seen situations like yours before. Their valuation isn't arbitrary.

Here are some realities worth keeping in mind.

Big verdicts mean something horrible happened to someone. A million-dollar settlement usually means catastrophic, life-altering injuries. It's not something to hope for.

You haven't won the lottery. A settlement compensates you for real losses—medical bills, lost wages, pain and suffering. It's not a windfall.

If you can still work after your injury, you're going to need to keep working after your settlement. The money is meant to make you whole, not to fund early retirement.

The cases you see on the news made the news for a reason. They're rare. They're noteworthy. And they're often misunderstood or misrepresented in the coverage.

Talk to your attorney about valuation. Ask questions. But approach the conversation with realistic expectations—and with an understanding of the particular dynamics that affect premises liability cases in New Mexico.

Making the Partnership Work

The best outcomes happen when attorney and client work as a team. Your attorney brings legal knowledge, experience, and systems. You bring the facts of your situation, responsiveness, and honesty.

Keep communication open. Respond to requests. Tell the truth, even when it's uncomfortable. Understand that the process takes time. Ask questions when you don't understand something.

Do those things, and you'll be the kind of client attorneys love to work with—and you'll put yourself in the best position for a successful outcome.

PART 2

UNDERSTANDING YOUR CASE

You have the foundation in place. You know what makes premises cases different. You've found an attorney you trust. You understand the fee arrangement and what the working relationship should look like.

Now comes the work.

Part II takes you inside the mechanics of a slip, trip, and fall claim. This is where we get into the questions that will shape your case: Who is legally responsible for your injuries? What evidence do you need, and how do you preserve it? What is your case actually worth? How do settlement negotiations work? What happens if your case goes to court?

Some of these chapters address issues you'll face in almost any premises case. Liability—the question of who was at fault and why—is fundamental. So is evidence preservation, medical treatment, and case valuation. You'll want to understand these regardless of your specific situation.

Other chapters address circumstances that may or may not apply to you. If your fall happened on government property, Chapter 11 explains the special rules under the New Mexico Tort Claims Act. If you're a tenant injured in a rental property, or if your fall involves a landlord-tenant relationship, Chapter 12 covers that territory. If you're a Medicare recipient, Chapter 17 walks through the compliance requirements that affect your settlement. Read what applies. Skip what doesn't.

Throughout Part II, you'll see why premises cases require more investigation, more analysis, and often more litigation than a typical car accident claim. The property owner, the building owner, the tenant, the maintenance company, the municipality—any or all of them might share responsibility. Safety standards vary by industry and context. Expert witnesses may be needed to establish what went wrong and why. These complexities are why you need an attorney who understands premises liability specifically, and why your informed participation matters.

This part of the book won't make you a lawyer. But it will make you a better partner to your legal team. When your attorney explains why they're hiring a safety expert, you'll understand. When they discuss the challenges of proving notice, you'll follow the conversation. When a settlement offer arrives, you'll have context for evaluating whether it's fair.

That's the goal: not to do your attorney's job, but to understand it well enough to work together effectively. Let's get into it.

CHAPTER 8

HOW LIABILITY WORKS IN SLIPS, TRIPS, AND FALLS

This chapter covers the central question in any premises case: who is legally responsible for your injuries, and why?

Understanding liability matters because it shapes everything else. It determines whether you have a case at all. It influences what your case is worth. It affects settlement negotiations and, if necessary, how your case is presented to a jury.

Premises liability is more complex than car accident liability. There are few specific laws that clearly define who was right and who was wrong. Instead, we work with broader principles that apply differently depending on the circumstances. This chapter explains those principles.

The Standard of Care

New Mexico law requires property owners and occupants to exercise "ordinary care" to keep their premises reasonably safe for people who come onto the property.

That sounds straightforward. It isn't.

"Ordinary care" doesn't mean the same thing everywhere. What constitutes ordinary care varies with the nature of what is being done. In other words, the standard depends on the activity.

What's reasonable for a hospital is different from what's reasonable for a hiking trail. What's reasonable for a busy restaurant is different from what's reasonable for a quiet office building. What's reasonable for snow removal in Taos—where winter weather is a fact of life for months—is different from what's reasonable in parts of the state that receive less snow.

This context-dependence is what makes premises cases challenging. There are few bright-line rules. Instead, it's up to the lawyers to argue for what constitutes reasonable care in a given situation, and ultimately up to juries to decide whether the property owner met that standard.

What Counts as a Hazard?

Liability in most slip, trip, and fall cases focuses on the hazard—the physical condition or object that caused the fall. Before we can talk about fault, we need to establish that there was actually a dangerous condition that shouldn't have existed.

This is a threshold question, and it's not always obvious.

If you trip on an ordinary, well-maintained, code-compliant staircase, there's likely no liability. The staircase isn't a hazard just because you fell on it. Sometimes people fall and it's nobody's fault.

But subtle issues come up constantly. Consider floor mats. Many businesses place mats near entrances to prevent mud and water from spreading inside. The mat itself is hazard prevention. But if that mat gets folded over or bunched up, it becomes a tripping hazard. The same object can be safe or dangerous depending on its condition.

Whether something qualifies as a hazard is context-specific. A puddle in the middle of a grocery store aisle is almost certainly a hazard—water doesn't belong there, customers don't expect it, and the flooring is typically smooth and slippery when wet. But a puddle outside the showers in a gym locker room? People expect wet floors near showers. That same puddle might not be a hazard in that context.

In many cases, it takes an expert witness to establish whether a particular condition was actually dangerous. A safety expert can explain industry standards, evaluate the specific hazard, and help a jury understand why the condition was unreasonable. This is one of the ways premises cases become more expensive and complex than car accident cases.

Did the Responsible Party Know About the Hazard?

Once we establish that a hazard existed, the next question is whether the property owner or occupant knew about it.

If they knew about the hazard and failed to take reasonable action—either to fix it or to warn people about it—they may be liable. The key word is "reasonable." A cracked sidewalk can't necessarily be repaired the same day it's discovered. But the owner should act promptly to provide warnings: yellow paint over the crack, an orange cone, a sign. How much is enough? How much is too little? There are no hard and fast rules. That's what makes these cases challenging.

But what if they didn't know about the hazard? That doesn't automatically mean they avoid liability.

The question becomes: should they have known?

Property owners and occupants can't stick their heads in the sand. New Mexico law charges them with the responsibility to conduct reasonable inspections of their premises. If they fail to conduct reasonable inspections, the law treats them as if they knew about any hazard that a reasonable inspection would have revealed.

What's a Reasonable Inspection?

Again, it depends on the circumstances.

In an urban grocery store with hundreds or thousands of customers a day, reasonable inspections might mean having employees check the aisles every few minutes for spills. The combination of heavy foot traffic, smooth floors, and constant product handling creates ongoing risk. Frequent checks are the only way to catch hazards promptly.

In a different establishment—say, a small, quiet bookstore with far fewer customers—maybe a daily walkthrough is enough. The risk profile is different. The inspection schedule should match.

There's also a temporal element. How long was the hazard there before you fell? A spill that happened five minutes ago might be reasonable in some contexts—there simply wasn't time for an employee to discover it. But a spill that sat there for two hours? That's much harder to defend.

The time analysis works in conjunction with the nature of the activity. Ten minutes might be reasonable in a low-traffic office hallway. Ten minutes might be completely unreasonable in the produce section of a busy supermarket on a Saturday afternoon. It depends on the amount of foot traffic, the texture of the floor, the type of business, and frankly, simple social expectations about how that type of establishment should operate.

A company's own conduct can help establish what's reasonable. Say a property usually checks a certain hallway twice a day. But one day the regular employee calls in sick, management doesn't assign anyone else, and the hallway doesn't get checked at all. Then someone trips on debris. If the norm is twice a day and it wasn't done at all, that's likely not reasonable—by the company's own standards.

Proving Knowledge

How do we actually show that a property owner knew or should have known about a hazard? Several types of evidence come into play.

Prior complaints or incidents. If other people have complained about the same hazard, or if there have been previous falls in the same location, that's powerful evidence of knowledge. It shows the owner was on notice that a problem existed.

Employee testimony. Did any employees see the hazard before you fell? Were they aware of the condition? What did they do or not do about it?

Inspection documentation. Records showing when inspections occurred—and what they did or didn't note—can be revealing. If an employee walked through an area shortly before your fall and didn't document the hazard, that raises questions. Either the inspection wasn't thorough, or the hazard developed after the inspection (which affects the time analysis).

Internal communications. Emails or messages where employees asked management, "Are we going to get this fixed?" Work orders that were created but never completed. Requests made to corporate that weren't followed through on. These documents show that the organization was aware of a problem and failed to address it.

The company's own policies. If a company had a policy requiring certain actions—cleaning on a certain schedule, responding to spills within a certain time, inspecting at certain intervals—and failed to follow that policy, it cuts against them. They set the standard and didn't meet it.

Industry standards and regulations. Some circumstances fall under industry-specific regulations. OSHA requirements apply in many settings. Various industries have trade organizations that publish standards. Organizations like ANSI publish broadly applicable safety standards. If a property owner violated a relevant standard, that helps establish unreasonableness.

Common sense. Sometimes the strongest argument is an appeal to the jury's basic understanding of what's reasonable. A jury doesn't need an expert to tell them that a gaping hole in a walkway should have been repaired.

Few cases are cut and dry. Typically, your attorney evaluates the circumstances and builds a compelling case by weaving together several of these elements.

What About Warning Signs?

People often assume that a warning sign settles the question of liability. They think either "There was no sign, so they're liable" or "There was a sign, so they're protected."

Neither is true. A warning sign is one factor in the overall analysis—not a magic shield and not an automatic admission of fault.

A property owner who knows about a hazard has options: fix it, warn people about it, or both. Warning signs can be part of a reasonable response. If a spill just happened and an employee puts out a wet floor sign while someone else gets a mop, that's probably reasonable.

But a sign is not a substitute for fixing something that can be fixed. If a broken step has had a warning cone next to it for six months, the question becomes: why hasn't it been repaired? At some point, the sign stops being a reasonable temporary measure and starts looking like an excuse for inaction.

Whether a sign provided meaningful warning depends on the specifics. Placement matters—a sign behind you as you approach a hazard doesn't help. Visibility matters—a small sign in a dimly lit area isn't the same as a bright sign at eye level. Specificity matters—a generic "Caution" sign doesn't tell you what to watch for, while "Wet Floor" or "Step Down" communicates the actual danger. Readability, color, and the nature of the surrounding activity all factor in. What's adequate warning in a quiet office hallway might be insufficient in a busy store aisle where customers are focused on merchandise.

Warning signs most directly affect your case through comparative fault. If you saw a sign and proceeded anyway, that will likely increase your share of responsibility. This doesn't mean you automatically lose—the jury will consider whether you acted reasonably given the warning. If you didn't see the sign, the question shifts to whether it was placed and designed in a way that a reasonable person would have noticed it.

Your attorney will evaluate the specific circumstances: what the sign said, where it was placed, how visible it was, how long the hazard existed, and whether the property owner should have done more than just post a warning. Like everything else in premises liability, the answers depend on the facts.

Responsible Parties

Who exactly is responsible for maintaining safe conditions? The answer can be complicated.

In any given premises case, there may be multiple involved parties: the owner of the property, the tenant or occupant, a third-party maintenance company contracted to perform inspections or upkeep, and the municipality if a public sidewalk is involved.

Take a simple example. After a storm, there's a slick icy patch on the sidewalk in front of a clothing store.

Because it's a public sidewalk, the city or local government may be responsible for maintenance. But under New Mexico law, the adjacent property may also have a duty to clear ice and snow. So who does that mean?

The person who owns the building might have leased the storefront to another business. That's two potentially involved parties right there—the owner and the tenant. But what if one of them contracted with a separate maintenance company to handle snow and ice removal? Now there's a third potentially responsible party.

In some situations, there are multiple layers of leases, including subleases. There may be property management companies or condominium associations involved. It can get complicated quickly.

Chapter 9 covers the research tools and methods used to identify and name all these parties. For now, the important point is that premises cases often involve multiple defendants, and part of your attorney's job is to figure out who they all are.

Comparative Fault

New Mexico follows a comparative fault system. This means the jury compares the fault of all involved parties—including you, the injured person.

Why would you share fault for your own fall? Because New Mexico law holds that everyone has a responsibility to watch out for their own safety. If you were distracted and contributed to your fall—looking at your phone, not watching where you walked, ignoring an obvious hazard—the jury may assign some or even all of the fault to you.

Here's how it works in practice. The jury is given a list of all involved parties and instructed to assign a percentage of fault to each, adding up to 100%. There are literally blank lines on the verdict form where jurors write in percentages.

For example:

- Injured person: 15%
- Landowner: 50%
- Tenant: 35%
- City: 0%

Then the damages are allocated based on those percentages. If total damages are $100,000 and the above fault allocation applies, the landowner would be responsible for $50,000, the tenant for $35,000, and you would absorb $15,000 of your own losses.

This is why defense attorneys in premises cases almost always argue that the injured person shares fault. Every percentage point they can shift onto you reduces what their client has to pay. And as we discussed in Chapter 2, these arguments have more traction in fall cases than in car accident cases. Juries are often receptive to the idea that someone should have been watching where they were going.

Understanding comparative fault helps you understand why your attorney evaluates your case the way they do. If there's a reasonable chance a jury will put significant fault on you, that affects the realistic value of your claim—even if the property owner was clearly negligent.

Intoxication and Your Case

One factor that significantly complicates premises cases: intoxication.

If you had been drinking or using drugs before your fall, your case becomes much more challenging. It's not an absolute bar to recovery—you can still have a valid claim if the property owner was negligent. But intoxication is a strong factor that weighs heavily in the mix of all the other considerations.

Here's why. Remember that the defense will almost always argue you share fault for your fall. They'll say you should have been watching where you were going, should have seen the hazard, should have avoided it. Now add intoxication to the picture. The argument writes itself: you fell because you were impaired, not because of any hazard. Your judgment was affected. Your balance was compromised. You weren't capable of exercising ordinary care for your own safety.

Juries are receptive to this argument. If evidence shows you were intoxicated—blood alcohol results from the ER, witness testimony about your behavior, your own admissions—expect the defense to use it aggressively. Even if a genuine hazard existed, a jury may assign a large share of fault to you based on your condition.

This doesn't mean you should hide information about intoxication from your attorney. The opposite is true. Your attorney needs to know so they can evaluate your case realistically and prepare for how the defense will use it. Surprises at trial are far worse than difficult facts addressed early.

If intoxication is part of your situation, be honest with your attorney. They can assess how it affects your case and whether a path forward still makes sense.

Waivers and Releases of Liability

A word about waivers. It's increasingly common for businesses to require customers to sign a waiver or release of liability before participating in certain activities. These documents are written broadly, attempting to bar any injury claim you might bring against the business.

What does New Mexico law say about these waivers?

The general rule is this: waivers and releases are enforceable, but only as to risks inherent in the activity.

Here's an example. You sign up for a martial arts class and sign a waiver saying you can't sue for any injury sustained in the class. During sparring, you take a hard kick, fall, and break your wrist. That seems like a risk inherent in the sport. The waiver is likely enforceable.

But take a different scenario. A staff member mops the studio floor and leaves a puddle. You slip in the puddle, fall, and break your wrist. Same injury, but slipping on a puddle from mopping is probably not a risk inherent in martial arts. You might be able to pursue a claim despite the waiver.

Of course, you can imagine examples that fall somewhere in between. What about a wet spot from someone's water bottle during class? What about equipment that wasn't properly maintained? These situations get fact-specific quickly.

Most slip and fall cases involve establishments open to the public—stores, restaurants, parking lots—where waivers aren't part of the picture. But waivers come up often enough, particularly with gyms, recreational facilities, and activity-based businesses, that you need to be aware of them.

The key point: just because you signed a waiver doesn't mean you have no claim. The waiver needs to be examined and analyzed in light of the specific circumstances of your injury. If the hazard that caused your fall wasn't an inherent risk of the activity you signed up for, the waiver may not protect the business.

The Big Picture

Liability in premises cases is rarely simple. The standard of care varies by context. What counts as a hazard depends on the circumstances. Knowledge can be actual or constructive. Inspections must be reasonable—but reasonable means different things in different settings. Multiple parties may share responsibility. And the injured person's own conduct is always part of the analysis.

This complexity is exactly why these cases require careful investigation and often expert testimony. It's also why you need an attorney who understands premises liability specifically—not just injury law generally.

The good news is that complexity cuts both ways. A property owner can't escape liability just because the situation is complicated. Your attorney's job is to work through that complexity, gather the evidence, identify the responsible parties, and build the strongest possible case for why the property owner failed to meet their duty of care.

That's how premises cases are won.

CHAPTER 9

IDENTIFYING THE AT-FAULT PARTIES

The sign on the door is only a starting point. It's not the end of the investigation.

As we discussed in Chapter 8, premises cases often involve multiple responsible parties: the property owner, the building owner if different, the tenant or occupant, maintenance contractors, and potentially the municipality. Your attorney's job is to identify all of them. Miss one and you might miss the insurance coverage that would actually pay your claim.

This chapter walks through how that investigation works. You won't be doing this yourself—this is work for your attorney and their staff—but understanding the process helps you appreciate why premises cases require more legwork than a typical car accident claim.

Why This Matters for the Statute of Limitations

Before we get into the research methods, an important point about timing.

The statute of limitations runs independently for each party you want to sue. The fact that you filed suit against the property owner in time does not mean you can automatically bring in the tenant company or a maintenance contractor later.

This is why you shouldn't wait until the statute of limitations is nearly exhausted to begin your case. What if discovery reveals another responsible party? You need time to amend your complaint and add them. If the limitations period has already run on that party, you're out of luck—even if you only just learned they existed.

Start early. Identify as many parties as possible before litigation. But recognize that sometimes it takes discovery to uncover all of them, and build in time for that possibility.

The Comparative Fault Problem

Here's why identifying all responsible parties isn't just important—it's essential.

Remember the comparative fault example from Chapter 8? The jury assigns a percentage of fault to every party who had a duty of care, and your recovery is reduced by your own share of fault. Here's the part that catches people off guard: the jury can assign fault to any party who had a duty—even parties you didn't sue, or couldn't sue because the statute of limitations ran out.

Think about what that means. Say you sue the property owner, but you missed the deadline to sue the maintenance company that was actually responsible for the hazard. At trial, the property owner's attorney argues that the maintenance company was really at fault. The jury agrees and assigns 70% of the fault to the maintenance company.

You can't collect from the maintenance company—they're not in the lawsuit. And the property owner is only responsible for their 30% share. If your damages were $100,000, you recover $30,000 instead of $100,000. The other $70,000 disappears.

This is why thorough investigation matters so much. Every responsible party you fail to identify and sue is a party the defense can point to and shift blame onto—knowing you can't recover from them. Identifying all parties isn't just about having more defendants. It's about making sure you can actually collect on the fault that's assigned.

Starting with What's Visible

The investigation begins with what you can see.

The name on the sign tells you what the business calls itself publicly. But that name may or may not be the legal entity that operates the location. It could be a trade name—a "doing business as" or d/b/a—used by a company with a completely different legal name. Or it could be a franchise location operated by a local company under a national brand.

The franchise question matters. If a location is a franchise, the national brand you recognize—the name on the sign—is typically not the party responsible for day-to-day operations and premises maintenance. Instead, a local franchisee company operates the location. That's the entity your attorney needs to identify and name.

Does the franchisor ever share liability? It's possible, depending on the franchisor's policies and level of control over operations. But typically, only the local operator is responsible for conditions at that specific location.

Business Registration Records

Once the visible name is identified, the next step is tracing it to a legal entity.

Your attorney can search business registration data through the New Mexico Secretary of State's office to find corporate filings. This reveals the legal name of the company, when it was formed, and who its registered agent is.

Local business licenses can also be helpful, sometimes more so than state records. A city or county business license identifies who is actually permitted to operate at that location. For franchises especially, local licensing may be the better path to identifying the specific company running the establishment.

Property Records

Who owns the land and building where you fell? That's often a different entity than the business operating there.

County records—tax assessment data, recorded deeds, and property transfer documents—identify the landowner. Your attorney pulls these records to determine who holds title to the property.

The owner might be an individual, a family trust, a limited liability company, or a large commercial real estate firm. Whoever it is, they may have duties related to the property's condition—especially for common areas, structural issues, or exterior hazards like sidewalks and parking lots.

If the property owner leased the space to an operating business, there may be a lease agreement that allocates maintenance responsibilities between them. Your attorney will want to see that document, though it typically isn't available until discovery.

Court Records

Has this property owner, business, or location been involved in prior litigation? Court records can reveal useful information.

If the same parties have been sued before—especially for similar incidents—those case files may identify affiliated companies, management structures, insurance carriers, or other details that inform your case. Prior lawsuits can also establish notice: if a property owner was sued years ago for the same type of hazard and failed to fix it, that's powerful evidence.

Your attorney can search court records at both the state and federal level to see what's out there.

Public Records Requests

Government agencies hold information that can help identify responsible parties and establish the history of a property.

Permit applications for construction, renovation, or repair work identify the contractors involved. If your fall resulted from a defect connected to recent construction—a poorly installed floor, a ramp that doesn't meet code—the contractor who did the work may share responsibility.

Licensing files, inspection records, and code enforcement documents can also be revealing. A history of violations or complaints puts the property owner on notice of problems.

Your attorney can obtain these documents through public records requests to state and local agencies.

When Government Entities Are Involved

If your investigation reveals that a government entity may be responsible—the city owns the sidewalk, the state operates the building, a public school district controls the property—everything changes.

The New Mexico Tort Claims Act imposes special rules for claims against government entities. The statute of limitations is shorter. And critically, there are notice requirements that must be met very early in the process. Miss the notice deadline and your claim against the government may be barred entirely, regardless of how strong it is.

This is why early investigation matters so much. If your attorney doesn't identify government involvement until months into the case, it may already be too late to pursue that party. The TCA deadlines are unforgiving.

Chapter 11 covers government property claims in detail. For now, the key point is this: whenever the investigation suggests a government entity might be involved, your attorney should immediately evaluate the TCA implications.

Other Research Tools

Sometimes the investigation uses simpler methods.

Good old-fashioned internet searches can turn up useful information. News articles about the business, online reviews mentioning safety issues, corporate websites explaining ownership structures—you never know what might surface.

Online maps can help too. If multiple businesses are listed at the same address, are they related? Is there a property management company involved? A shared landlord?

Professional databases that aggregate business information can fill in gaps about corporate relationships, registered agents, and affiliated entities.

None of these tools are magic. But layered together, they help build a picture of who controls the property and who might share responsibility for its condition.

What Litigation Reveals

Your attorney tries to identify as many parties as possible before filing suit. But some information simply isn't available until litigation begins.

Internal documents—lease agreements, maintenance contracts, inspection logs, corporate communications—typically can't be obtained without the formal discovery process. Once a lawsuit is filed, your attorney can use interrogatories, requests for production, and depositions to get these materials.

Discovery might reveal that a maintenance company was responsible for the area where you fell. Or that the property owner contracted out inspections to a third party. Or that the business had a corporate policy on hazard response that wasn't being followed.

If discovery identifies a new responsible party, your attorney can move to amend the complaint and add them—assuming the statute of limitations hasn't run. This is why timing matters. You need room in the schedule for the investigation to unfold.

The Goal

The goal of all this work is simple: identify everyone who might share responsibility for the conditions that caused your fall.

Some of those parties will have insurance. Some may not. Some may have significant assets. Others may be judgment-proof. Your attorney evaluates each one and decides who to pursue.

In some cases, the answer is straightforward—a single business clearly controlled the property and the hazard. In others, there are layers of owners, tenants, contractors, and possibly government entities, each with their own potential exposure.

The investigation is how you find out which situation you're in. And it's why premises cases require an attorney who knows where to look.

CHAPTER 10

PRESERVING EVIDENCE

Chapter 1 covered what to do immediately after a fall: photograph the hazard, get witness information, request an incident report. Those steps matter because you're capturing evidence while it's still available.

This chapter is about what comes next—the ongoing work of preserving evidence throughout your case. Much of this falls on your attorney, not you. But understanding the process helps you appreciate why moving quickly matters, and why the early investigation work we discussed in Chapter 9 is so important.

Why Evidence Disappears

Evidence in premises cases has a way of vanishing.

Hazards get fixed. Once a fall occurs, property owners often correct the problem quickly. That's good for public safety—but it means the physical evidence of what caused your fall may be gone within hours. The wet floor gets mopped. The broken tile gets replaced. The cracked sidewalk gets repaired. Without photographs from the scene, you may have no proof the hazard ever existed.

Surveillance footage gets overwritten. Many businesses have security cameras, and those cameras may have captured your fall. But most systems only store footage for a limited time—days or weeks—before recording over it. If no one asks the business to preserve that footage, it disappears automatically.

Documents get lost or destroyed. Inspection logs, maintenance records, incident reports—these exist somewhere in the business's files, but businesses don't keep everything forever. Records get purged. Files get lost. Systems get updated and old data doesn't transfer.

Employees leave. The person who mopped the floor, the manager who responded to your fall, the maintenance worker who was supposed to inspect the area—any of them might quit, get fired, or transfer to another location. The longer time passes, the harder it becomes to identify and locate the people who know what happened.

Time is not on your side. The evidence you need to prove your case is most available immediately after the incident. Every day that passes, something else may disappear.

Preservation Letters

Your attorney's primary tool for protecting evidence is the preservation letter.

A preservation letter is a formal notice sent to the property owner, business, or other potentially responsible party. It informs them that a claim may be coming and demands that they preserve all evidence related to the incident.

What gets requested? Typically everything that might be relevant:

- Surveillance footage from cameras in and around the area of the fall
- Incident or accident reports completed at the time
- Maintenance logs and inspection records
- Employee schedules showing who was working that day
- Training records for employees involved in maintenance or hazard response
- Policy manuals covering safety inspections, spill response, and hazard correction
- Emails, text messages, or other communications about the hazard or the incident
- Work orders or repair requests related to the area where you fell
- Prior complaints or incident reports involving similar hazards

The letter puts the recipient on notice that this evidence must be kept. It creates a record that they knew a claim existed and knew they had a duty to preserve relevant materials.

The Limits of Preservation Letters

A preservation letter is not a subpoena. It doesn't give you the right to access the evidence—not yet. Before litigation, you typically can't force a business to hand over their internal documents. That requires the formal discovery process, which only becomes available after a lawsuit is filed.

What a preservation letter does is establish the duty to preserve. The recipient can't claim they didn't know a claim was coming. They can't say they routinely delete footage after two weeks and yours just happened to get erased. The letter takes those excuses off the table.

If the recipient destroys evidence after receiving a preservation letter, they may face sanctions from the court. Whether sanctions are actually imposed is highly discretionary—it depends on the judge, and some judges are reluctant to grant them. To get sanctions, you typically need to show that you were prejudiced by the destruction. That puts the claimant in a difficult position: how do you prove you were harmed by missing evidence when you don't know what that evidence would have shown?

In practice, even when formal sanctions aren't granted, your attorney can argue to the jury that the defense destroyed evidence and ask the jury to draw conclusions from that. If a business received a preservation letter and then "lost" the surveillance footage, jurors may infer they were trying to hide something.

The preservation letter is both a practical tool and a strategic one. It protects evidence when the other side acts in good faith, and it creates consequences when they don't.

Moving Fast

Preservation letters only work if they arrive in time.

Surveillance footage that records over itself every seven days is gone on day eight. A preservation letter sent on day ten does nothing. The evidence is already destroyed—and the business can honestly say they never received notice to keep it.

This is why the party identification work we discussed in Chapter 9 matters so much. You can't send a preservation letter to a party you haven't identified. If it takes weeks to figure out that a maintenance company was responsible for the area where you fell, that's weeks of potential evidence loss.

Your attorney should send preservation letters as soon as responsible parties are identified. For obvious parties—the business operating at the location, the property owner—letters should go out almost immediately. For parties discovered later through investigation, letters should follow as soon as they're identified.

Speed costs very little. A preservation letter is a straightforward document. Sending one takes minimal time and expense. The potential benefit—saving evidence that might otherwise vanish—is enormous.

What If Time Has Already Passed?

Maybe you're reading this weeks or months after your fall. Maybe you didn't hire an attorney right away. Maybe the attorney you hired didn't move as quickly as they should have.

Is it too late to send preservation letters?

Send them anyway.

You never know what might still exist. Some businesses keep footage longer than others. Some maintain detailed records going back years. Employee records and policy manuals may still be available even if the specific incident documentation is gone.

A preservation letter sent late is still better than no letter at all. It costs almost nothing to send, and it can only help. At worst, the evidence is already gone. At best, you preserve something that would otherwise have been lost.

Don't assume nothing remains just because time has passed. Let your attorney make that determination after doing everything possible to preserve what's left.

Government Defendants and Public Records

If a government entity may be responsible for your fall—the city, the state, a public school district—your attorney has an additional tool: public records requests.

Government agencies are subject to public records laws that require them to produce documents in response to proper requests. Unlike private businesses, where you typically need litigation to access internal records, government records can often be obtained before any lawsuit is filed.

This is valuable for several reasons. You can get inspection records, maintenance logs, prior complaints, and internal communications earlier in the process. You can evaluate the strength of your case against the government entity before committing to litigation. And you create a clear record of what existed at the time of your request—making it harder for documents to disappear later.

Of course, if a government entity is involved, the Tort Claims Act deadlines we've discussed throughout this book become critical. Public records requests are useful, but they don't substitute for meeting the TCA's strict notice requirements.

Employee Turnover

One challenge that preservation letters can't fully solve: people leave.

Businesses have turnover. The employee who witnessed your fall may quit six months later. The manager who was on duty that day may transfer to another location. The maintenance worker who was supposed to inspect the area may no longer work there by the time your case reaches litigation.

When employees leave, their knowledge goes with them. Your attorney can try to identify and locate former employees for depositions, but it's harder than deposing someone who still works at the company. Former employees may be difficult to find. They may be uncooperative. They may have forgotten details.

This is another reason why time matters. The sooner your attorney can identify key witnesses and lock in their testimony—through depositions or detailed statements—the better. Waiting until trial to talk to witnesses who may no longer be reachable is a risk.

Save Your Footwear

Here's something many people don't think about: your shoes are evidence.

In almost every fall case, the defense will ask about your footwear. What kind of shoes were you wearing? What condition were they in? Were the soles worn? Was the tread adequate? Were they appropriate for the conditions?

Your shoes can answer those questions—or they can become a problem if they're gone.

As soon as possible after your fall, take photographs of the footwear you were wearing. Photograph them from multiple angles, including the bottom to show the tread and sole condition. These photos document how your shoes looked at the time of the incident.

Then save the actual shoes. If you can, stop wearing them. Every time you wear them, you add wear and tear that wasn't there on the day you fell.

Keep the shoes somewhere safe where they won't get damaged, discarded, or lost. Let your attorney know you have them. They may need to be produced for inspection later in the case.

Whatever you do, don't throw them away. Discarding the shoes you were wearing when you fell could lead to accusations that you destroyed evidence. Even if you didn't mean anything by it—even if you just thought they were old shoes—the defense may argue you got rid of them because they would have hurt your case.

Save the shoes. It's simple, it costs nothing, and it removes a potential problem.

Your Role in Evidence Preservation

Most evidence preservation is your attorney's job. But there are a few things you can do.

Hold onto everything you have. The photographs you took at the scene, any paperwork you received, notes you made about what happened, contact information for witnesses—keep all of it safe and organized. Give copies to your attorney, but keep your own copies too. And as we just discussed, save the shoes you were wearing.

If you remember additional details or witnesses later, tell your attorney immediately. That person you just recalled who saw you fall? Your attorney may be able to track them down.

Follow your attorney's guidance about social media and public statements. Anything you post online may be discoverable. Don't give the other side ammunition.

The Bottom Line

Evidence preservation is a race against time. Footage gets overwritten. Hazards get fixed. Documents get lost. Employees leave. The longer you wait, the more you lose.

Your attorney's job is to identify responsible parties quickly and send preservation letters immediately. Your job is to hire an attorney who understands this urgency and acts on it.

The evidence that exists today may not exist tomorrow. Move fast.

CHAPTER 11

SLIPS, TRIPS, AND FALLS ON GOVERNMENT PROPERTY

If your fall occurred on government property, different rules apply. Miss the deadlines and your claim could be barred forever—even if the government was clearly at fault.

We've mentioned the New Mexico Tort Claims Act throughout this book. This chapter explains it in detail, along with the federal rules that apply when a federal entity is involved. If there's any possibility that a government body shares responsibility for your fall, read this chapter carefully.

Government Involvement Isn't Always Obvious

Sometimes it's clear you fell on government property. You slipped on ice outside a city building. You tripped on a broken sidewalk in front of a public school. You fell in a state park.

Other times, it's not obvious at all.

Private businesses sometimes rent space from government entities. A restaurant might operate in a building owned by the city. A shop might lease space in a county-owned development. The business looks private, but the underlying property belongs to a public body.

The reverse happens too. Government offices sometimes rent space from private landlords. A state agency might operate out of a privately owned office building.

And then there are the complicated arrangements. A building owned by a private party sits on land owned by the government under a long-term ground lease. A state entity leases land to a county. A private vendor operates a booth on government property during a public event. Public-private partnerships blur the lines at stadiums, convention centers, and event venues.

Public sidewalks are a common example. The city or municipality often has maintenance responsibilities for sidewalks, but so do the adjacent private property owners. A fall on a public sidewalk might involve claims against both.

This is why the party identification work we discussed in Chapter 9 is so critical. You need to know whether a government entity is involved early—because the deadlines for government claims are much shorter than for private parties.

Federal vs. State and Local

Different rules apply depending on whether the government entity is federal, state, or local.

Claims against federal entities fall under the Federal Tort Claims Act. Claims against state and local entities in New Mexico fall under the New Mexico Tort Claims Act. The procedures and deadlines are different.

Most premises cases involve state or local government, not federal. For most of us, daily life involves far more interaction with city and state property than federal property. But if your fall occurred on federal land, in a federal building, or involved a federal agency, you need to know the federal rules.

Federal Tort Claims Act

If a federal entity may be responsible for your fall, the Federal Tort Claims Act governs your claim.

The FTCA generally requires you to file an administrative claim within two years of the incident. This is not a lawsuit—it's a formal claim submitted to the federal agency. You must go through this administrative process as a precondition to filing suit. You cannot skip it and go directly to court.

After the agency denies your claim—or fails to respond within six months—you have a limited time to file suit in federal court.

The administrative requirement adds a layer of complexity that doesn't exist with state and local claims. Your attorney needs to identify federal involvement early and begin the administrative process promptly.

New Mexico Tort Claims Act

Far more common are claims involving state or local entities—cities, counties, state agencies, public schools, and similar bodies. These fall under the New Mexico Tort Claims Act.

The TCA has a critical requirement that trips up many claimants: you must provide written notice of your claim within 90 days of the incident.

Read that again. Ninety days. Not ninety days to file a lawsuit—ninety days to give notice that you may have a claim at all.

Within just three months of your fall, you need to have determined whether a state or local entity may be responsible for your injury. If you fail to give appropriate notice within that window, your claim against the government could be barred permanently. It doesn't matter how strong your case is. It doesn't matter how badly you were hurt. Miss the notice deadline and you may have no claim.

After proper notice is given, you generally have two years from the date of the incident to file suit. Unlike the Federal Tort Claims Act, you don't have to go through an administrative process before filing in court. But you absolutely must meet the notice requirement.

What Proper Notice Requires

The notice must inform the government entity of the time, place, and circumstances of your fall. It must put them on notice that litigation may result.

Some government agencies have specific forms for tort claims notices. If a form exists, it's often a good idea to use it. But your attorney can also write a letter that meets the statutory requirements.

Here's where it gets tricky: the notice must go to the correct government official. The Tort Claims Act specifies which officials must receive notice, and the requirements are different for different types of entities. State agencies have different designated officials than counties. Counties are different from cities. Cities are different from school districts.

If you send notice to the wrong official, you may have a problem—even if you sent it on time. This is an area where precision matters and mistakes can be fatal to your claim.

Your attorney should know exactly who needs to receive notice for the specific type of entity involved. This is not something to handle on your own.

Exceptions Are Extremely Limited

Are there any ways around the 90-day notice requirement if you miss it?

Technically, a few exceptions exist. But they're extremely limited and rarely available in practice.

Notice is not required if you sue a government employee individually rather than the entity itself. But to do that, you'd need to know the exact specific person responsible for the hazard—which is difficult to determine without the kind of investigation that takes time.

The time frames are extended if a death is involved.

The deadline can be extended to a limited degree if the injured person was incapacitated and physically unable to give notice.

But these exceptions are narrow. Don't count on them. Treat the 90-day deadline as absolute, because in most cases it effectively is.

Schools Are Government Entities

One thing people sometimes forget: public schools are government entities. If you fell at a public school—in the parking lot, on the grounds, inside the building—the Tort Claims Act applies.

This includes school districts, public universities, and community colleges. The 90-day notice requirement applies to all of them.

Sovereign Immunity and What Can Be Litigated

Government entities have what's called sovereign immunity—protection from being sued. The Tort Claims Act waives that immunity, but only for specific types of claims.

For premises cases, here's the key distinction: claims based on maintenance problems can generally be litigated. Claims based on design problems cannot.

What's the difference? A maintenance problem is a failure to keep the property in safe condition—not fixing a broken step, not clearing ice from a walkway, not repairing a damaged floor. A design problem is a flaw in how the property was originally designed or constructed—a staircase that was built with inadequate railings, a walkway that was designed with a slope that collects water.

If your fall resulted from a maintenance failure, you can likely pursue a claim under the TCA. If your fall resulted from a design defect, sovereign immunity may not be waived, and you may not be able to sue the government at all.

The line between maintenance and design isn't always clear. Some situations could be characterized either way. This is an area where you need to discuss the specifics with your attorney to understand what your claim will really look like and whether it can proceed.

Damages Caps

Even if you successfully prove your claim against a government entity, your recovery may be limited.

The New Mexico Tort Claims Act imposes caps on damages. The exact amount you can recover depends on your medical bills and the damages awarded in various categories. Your attorney can explain how the caps apply to your specific situation.

These caps don't exist for claims against private parties. They're another way that government claims are different—and potentially less valuable—than similar claims against private defendants.

The Bottom Line

If there's any possibility that a government entity shares responsibility for your fall, time is critical.

You have 90 days to give notice under the New Mexico Tort Claims Act. That's three months to identify government involvement, determine the correct entity, figure out which official must receive notice, and get that notice delivered. Miss the deadline and your claim may be gone forever.

This is why we've emphasized throughout this book the importance of early investigation and prompt party identification. You can't give notice to an entity you haven't identified. You can't meet a deadline you don't know applies to you.

If you fell on what might be government property—or property with any government connection—tell your attorney immediately. Don't assume the business you see is the only party involved. Let your attorney investigate and determine whether the TCA applies.

The 90-day clock starts running the moment you fall. It doesn't wait for you to figure things out.

CHAPTER 12

LANDLORD/TENANT SITUATIONS

Falls at rental properties raise questions that don't exist when a single party owns and operates a location. Who's responsible—the landlord, the tenant, or both? The answer depends on where you fell, what caused your fall, and what the lease says about maintenance responsibilities.

This chapter covers the basics. Whether you're a tenant injured on your own rental property or a visitor injured at someone else's, understanding how responsibility gets divided helps you know what kind of case you might have.

Start with the Lease

The lease agreement is the starting point for any landlord/tenant premises case. Your attorney needs to see it.

The lease typically spells out who is responsible for maintaining what. Some responsibilities fall on the landlord. Others fall on the tenant. The specific terms vary from lease to lease, which is why you can't rely on general assumptions.

That said, some general principles apply in most situations.

Inside the Unit vs. Common Areas

The first big question is where the fall occurred.

Inside the rental unit. Hazards inside your own unit are generally your responsibility as a tenant. If you slip on a spill you created in your kitchen, that's not the landlord's fault. You control the space. You're responsible for keeping it safe.

The exception is when the hazard involves something the landlord is responsible for under the lease—and you requested a repair that the landlord failed to make. Say your lease makes the landlord responsible for plumbing, and a pipe has been leaking under your sink for weeks. You reported it. The landlord didn't fix it. You slip on the water that's been accumulating. That's a different situation. The landlord may be liable because they had a duty to repair, received notice, and failed to act.

Common areas. Hallways, stairwells, lobbies, parking lots, sidewalks, laundry rooms—these are generally the landlord's responsibility to maintain. Tenants don't control these spaces and can't be expected to fix hazards there.

But read your lease carefully. Depending on the nature of your building and unit, you may have some responsibility for areas adjacent to your unit—a porch, a patio, a small yard. The lease may assign maintenance duties for those spaces to you.

What Counts as Reasonable Response Time

If you report a hazard to your landlord, how long do they have to fix it before they're considered negligent?

There's no standard timeframe written into law. Like so much else in premises liability, it comes down to reasonableness under the circumstances.

The nature of the hazard matters enormously. Ice accumulating on exterior stairs? That needs to be addressed immediately—within hours, not days. It's an obvious danger that could cause serious injury at any moment.

A small gap at a door threshold? There may be more leeway. It's less immediately dangerous, and repairs might reasonably take longer to schedule.

The question is always what a reasonable property owner would do under the circumstances. Your attorney evaluates the specific hazard, how long the landlord knew about it, and what response would have been appropriate.

Claims by Tenants Against Landlords

If you're a tenant and you were injured due to your landlord's negligence, you can pursue a claim against them.

Some tenants worry that their lease might prevent this—that they signed something waiving their right to sue. Generally, a landlord cannot enforce a blanket waiver of liability for their own negligence. They have a legal duty to maintain common areas and to address hazards they're responsible for under the lease. They can't simply contract that duty away.

That doesn't mean your lease is irrelevant. The specific terms may affect what the landlord was responsible for and whether they breached that responsibility. But having signed a lease doesn't mean you've given up your right to pursue a legitimate injury claim.

Your attorney will review the lease terms and advise you on how they affect your situation.

Visitors at Rental Properties

What if you weren't the tenant—you were visiting someone at their rental property and you fell?

As a visitor, you may have claims against the landlord, the tenant, or both. It depends on where you fell, what caused your fall, and each party's respective duties.

If you fell in a common area due to a hazard the landlord should have addressed, the landlord may be liable. If you fell inside your friend's unit due to a hazard your friend created or failed to address, the tenant may be liable. If the hazard involves overlapping responsibilities—say, a porch that the tenant was supposed to maintain but the landlord knew was deteriorating—both may share liability.

This is similar to the multi-party situations we discussed in Chapters 8 and 9, where a landowner and a business tenant might both bear responsibility for a fall. The analysis is the same: identify all parties with potential duties, examine what each was responsible for, and determine who failed to meet their obligations.

Commercial vs. Residential Contexts

Here's something worth understanding about how these cases play out in practice.

If you look at the jury instructions, you'll see that everyone—whether a commercial landlord, a residential landlord, or an individual tenant—is held to the same basic standard: the duty to exercise "ordinary care" to keep premises reasonably safe for visitors.

But what constitutes ordinary care is highly contextual. It's shaped by social expectations, industry standards, and common sense—factors that aren't defined precisely in law but that judges, juries, and experts apply when evaluating a case.

As a practical matter, more is expected from commercial establishments that invite the public in for business purposes than from residential settings with limited visitors.

Think about it this way. There are things you accept in your own home or a friend's apartment that would be unacceptable hazards at a big-box retailer. A laptop charging cord stretched across a hallway. A small rug that's slightly bunched. A few items on the floor near a closet. In someone's home, these are normal parts of life. At a store with hundreds of customers, any of them could be a serious liability.

Why the difference? Commercial establishments put far more people at risk. They profit from inviting the public onto their premises. They have resources and systems to address hazards. The law holds everyone to "ordinary care," but ordinary care means something different when you're operating a business that sees hundreds of visitors a day versus hosting a friend for dinner.

This doesn't mean residential landlords have no duties. They absolutely do, especially in common areas. But if you're comparing a fall at a retail store in a strip mall to a fall while visiting a friend's apartment, the commercial context generally creates stronger expectations—and a stronger case.

Strip Malls, Shopping Centers, and Multi-Tenant Commercial Properties

Commercial rental properties—strip malls, shopping centers, office buildings—involve the same landlord/tenant analysis but with commercial stakes.

The property owner typically maintains common areas: parking lots, sidewalks, shared hallways, exterior lighting. Individual business tenants maintain their own spaces. But the lease controls, and commercial leases can allocate responsibilities in various ways.

If you fell in a parking lot, the property owner is probably responsible. If you fell inside a store, the store's operator is probably responsible. If you fell in a walkway right outside a store, it might depend on where exactly the landlord's responsibility ends and the tenant's begins.

These situations often involve the kind of multi-party analysis we've discussed throughout this book. Your attorney traces the responsible parties, examines the lease, and determines who had the duty to address the hazard that caused your fall.

The Bottom Line

Landlord/tenant situations add a layer of complexity to premises cases, but the fundamental analysis is the same: who had a duty, what were they responsible for, and did they fail to meet that responsibility?

The lease is the roadmap. Where you fell matters. What caused your fall matters. And whether you're a tenant or a visitor affects whose duties are at issue.

If you were injured at a rental property—residential or commercial—your attorney needs to see the lease and understand the specific allocation of responsibilities. Only then can they determine who to pursue and how to build your case.

CHAPTER 13

MEDICAL TREATMENT AND YOUR CLAIM

Medical treatment is at the heart of your injury claim. It's not just about getting better—though that matters most. Your treatment history is also the primary evidence of what happened to you, how badly you were hurt, and what you lost as a result.

Understanding the relationship between treatment and your claim helps you make better decisions about your care and avoid mistakes that could undermine your case.

How Treatment Affects What You Can Recover

New Mexico law allows injured people to recover damages in several categories. These come from the jury instructions that govern trials, but they also guide settlement negotiations at every stage. The categories include past and future medical expenses, past and future pain and suffering, past and future loss of enjoyment of life, the nature of the injury itself including disfigurement, and lost income.

Medical treatment figures into all of these, either directly or indirectly.

Medical expenses are straightforward. The cost of treatment—past bills and anticipated future care—is a direct component of damages.

Pain and suffering is harder to quantify. Medical treatment isn't the only measure of pain, but it's a widespread proxy. From a practical standpoint, more treatment is a rough indication that someone suffered more pain. That's not always perfectly true, but it's generally how adjusters, attorneys, and juries think about it.

Loss of enjoyment of life works similarly. More treatment suggests more disruption to your daily activities, your hobbies, your relationships. Treatment history becomes evidence of what you couldn't do while you were recovering.

Nature of the injury and disfigurement are also supported by treatment records. Surgeries, procedures, and ongoing care document the severity and lasting effects of what happened.

Lost income connects to treatment too. Your medical records help establish whether you could work during recovery, and for how long you were unable to earn a living.

The Threshold: Related, Necessary, and Reasonable

Not all medical treatment counts toward your claim. To figure into your damages, treatment must meet three criteria.

Related to the fall. The injury must have resulted from your fall or been aggravated—made worse—by it. Treatment for conditions unrelated to the incident doesn't count.

Necessary. The treatment must have been medically necessary as a result of your injury. Unnecessary procedures or excessive care don't contribute to your damages.

Reasonable. The cost must be reasonable for the treatment provided. If a single outpatient follow-up appointment costs $15,000, that's not reasonable, and it won't be counted at full value.

If your treatment is related, necessary, and reasonable, it supports your claim across all the damage categories. If it fails any of these tests, it becomes a problem.

Common Mistakes with Medical Treatment

People make predictable mistakes with their medical treatment that end up hurting their claims.

Waiting too long to seek treatment. This is the biggest one. People think their injuries will resolve on their own. They believe it's not that bad, or they can tough it out. Then things get worse, and they finally see a doctor—weeks or months after the fall.

That initial gap creates problems. The defense will argue that your injuries must have come from something else, not the fall. Or that you're exaggerating. Or that your sudden need for treatment was prompted by a lawyer getting involved, not by genuine injury.

As we discussed in Chapter 1, falls can be embarrassing. The natural impulse is to brush it off and move on. But if you're hurt, get checked out. If it's truly something minor that will resolve on its own, there's little harm in having had it evaluated. But if it turns out to be more serious, you'll be glad you went early.

Not following through on treatment. When you miss appointments, ignore your doctor's recommendations, or skip home exercises your physical therapist assigned, you undermine your case. The defense will point to your non-compliance and argue that you must not have been that injured, or that your failure to follow medical advice is why you're not better.

Follow doctor's orders. Do the exercises. Show up for appointments. This matters for your health and for your claim.

Gaps in treatment. Sometimes people treat for a while, start feeling better, stop treatment, and then get worse again. This happens—healing isn't linear. But gaps in your treatment history create obstacles.

Depending on the circumstances and the size of the case, we may bring in pain specialists or other experts to explain why the gap occurred. But it's not ideal. If you're still experiencing symptoms, keep treating. If your doctor says you can stop, document that it was their recommendation.

Choosing Providers

Even though this is an injury case, you're often still relying on your regular health insurance to pay for treatment before your case settles. That means your choices are constrained by your insurance network—whether you can go straight to a specialist depends on your plan, your HMO rules, and your referral requirements.

Navigating health insurance could fill its own book. But the advice I give is simple: follow your primary care doctor's recommendations for follow-up care, specialists, and referrals. Let them guide you through the system. If they recommend a specialist, see that specialist. If they recommend physical therapy, do physical therapy.

Don't try to engineer your treatment choices around what you think will help your claim. Get the care you need, when you need it, from the providers your doctor recommends.

Your Medical Records Will Be Used

Everything you say to medical providers can end up in your records. Those records will be reviewed by insurance adjusters, by attorneys, and potentially by a jury. Keep that in mind.

Be honest about everything. Don't try to manipulate the system through what you tell your doctors. The things people do to game the system usually hurt them more than they help.

Some intake forms ask directly: is this the result of an accident? Be honest. Think about what checking "no" will mean later when your medical records are reviewed. I don't know why people check "no" when they were injured in a fall—maybe concern about insurance or discomfort with the claims process—but it creates a problem for your case.

If a provider makes an incorrect note, try to get it corrected. Medical records sometimes contain errors. Maybe the doctor wrote down the wrong date, or recorded a symptom you didn't report, or got the mechanism of injury wrong. If you notice an error, point it out and ask for a correction. It doesn't always happen, but it's important to try.

The bottom line: be as honest and forthcoming as you can at every stage, and let the chips fall where they do. Honesty protects you better than any attempt to manage the narrative.

Pre-Existing Conditions

What if you had back problems before the fall, and the fall made them worse? Pre-existing conditions complicate things, but they don't eliminate your claim.

Under New Mexico law, you can still recover damages for the extent to which the fall aggravated a preexisting condition. If you had a bad back that was manageable before the incident and now requires surgery, the aggravation is compensable—even though you weren't starting from perfect health.

The challenge is figuring out how much of your current condition is pre-existing and how much resulted from the fall. In cases that justify it, we use medical experts to sort this out.

Here's how the principle works. Say you received $20,000 in treatment. Medical testimony establishes that your pre-existing condition accounted for 40% of your need for care, and the fall-related aggravation accounted for 60%. In that scenario, $12,000 would be attributable to your claim.

It rarely works out that neatly in real cases, but that's the concept. Pre-existing conditions don't bar recovery—they just require careful analysis of what the fall caused.

Be upfront about your medical history with both your providers and your attorney. Hiding a preexisting condition is far worse than disclosing it. Your attorney needs to know so they can address it properly.

Remember that if the claim goes to litigation, the attorneys on the other side can usually obtain medical records spanning years before the incident.

A Note on Fall-Related Injuries

As we discussed in Chapter 2, one challenge in premises cases is that juries don't intuitively understand how falls can cause serious injuries. A car crash involves obvious forces—two vehicles colliding at speed. A fall seems less violent.

But falls can cause severe and lasting damage. The human body is complex, and the severity of injury depends on angles, which body parts absorb impact, and countless other factors. Broken bones, herniated discs, torn ligaments, traumatic brain injuries—all of these can result from a fall.

Your medical records are the evidence that connects your fall to your injuries. Consistent, well-documented treatment helps establish that connection. Gaps and inconsistencies give the defense room to argue that your injuries came from somewhere else, or aren't as serious as you claim.

This is another reason why prompt, consistent treatment matters—not just for your recovery, but for proving your case.

Keep Good Records

One practical thing you can do to help your case: keep track of which providers and clinics you've visited. Names, addresses, dates of appointments.

Your attorney's office will need to gather all your medical records and bills to build your claim. Having a clear list of where you've been makes this process faster and reduces the chance that something gets missed.

You don't need to do anything elaborate. A simple list on your phone or a piece of paper works fine. Just note each provider as you go.

The Bottom Line

Your medical treatment tells the story of your injury. It documents what happened to you, how it affected your life, and what it cost to address.

Get treatment promptly. Follow through on what your doctors recommend. Be honest with your providers. Keep track of where you've been.

The better your treatment history reflects the reality of your injury, the stronger your claim will be.

CHAPTER 14

GETTING YOUR BILLS PAID WHILE YOUR CASE IS PENDING

Your case might take months to resolve. It might take years. Meanwhile, medical bills arrive in the mail. Providers want to be paid. Collection agencies start calling.

This is one of the most stressful parts of an injury claim—managing your financial obligations while waiting for a settlement that hasn't happened yet. This chapter explains your options and what you need to understand about how bills get handled.

There's No Single Timeline

People always want to know how long their case will take. The honest answer is that it depends.

Several factors affect the timeline. How severe are your injuries? How long does treatment take? How cooperative is the insurance company? Is liability contested? How backed up are the courts?

As we discussed in Chapter 2, premises cases often involve more contested liability than car accident cases. The property owner's insurance company may fight harder, which can stretch things out. A carrier that disputes responsibility or questions your injuries can extend the process through negotiation, litigation, and appeals.

Plan for your case to take longer than you'd like. Hope for faster, but don't count on it.

Options for Paying Medical Bills

While your case is pending, you have a few ways to handle medical expenses.

Health insurance. If you have health insurance through an employer, the marketplace, or a government program, use it. This is typically the best option. Your health insurance will pay for injury-related treatment just like it pays for any other medical care.

There's a catch, which we'll discuss in a moment. But for now, understand that health insurance is usually the most practical way to get treatment while your case is pending.

Health insurance plans have negotiated contractual rates with in-network providers. When you use health insurance, you get those lower rates. This matters because lower rates mean less money coming out of your eventual settlement to cover medical expenses.

Letters of protection. Some providers are willing to treat you now and wait for payment until your case settles. This arrangement is typically documented in a "letter of protection"—a letter from your attorney promising to pay the provider from your settlement in exchange for treatment.

Not all providers work this way. Chiropractors and some physical therapists often accept letters of protection. Most hospitals, surgeons, and other medical providers do not. They want to be paid through insurance or up front.

Letters of protection can help you access treatment when you don't have other options. But understand that the bills are accumulating, and they'll come out of your settlement at the end.

Out of pocket. If you don't have health insurance and can't find providers who will work on a letter of protection, you may need to pay out of pocket and seek reimbursement from your settlement later. This is the least desirable option, but sometimes it's the only one available.

Subrogation: The Surprise That Catches People

Here's something that surprises many people. If your health insurance pays for injury-related treatment, they expect to be paid back from your settlement.

This is called subrogation. It's a long-standing legal principle that applies in most states, including New Mexico. The concept is straightforward: if a negligent party caused the insurance company to pay for your medical care, the insurance company has a right to recover that money from whatever you collect from that party.

When your case settles, your health insurer will assert a subrogation claim. They'll want reimbursement for what they paid.

The good news is that subrogation claims are often negotiable. For various legal reasons, the amount the health insurer can recover is not necessarily dollar-for-dollar what they paid. There are opportunities to reduce the subrogation amount. But the health insurer does have a right to recover something.

This means your settlement won't all be yours to keep. A portion will go back to your health insurance company to reimburse them for injury-related care.

Liens Work Similarly

Sometimes a hospital or clinic will provide treatment and file a lien on your case rather than billing your insurance. A lien is a legal claim against your settlement—the provider is saying they're owed money from whatever you recover.

Like subrogation, liens get paid from your settlement at the end of the case. The provider waits for payment, but they have a legally enforceable right to collect.

If a provider files a lien, your attorney needs to know about it so it can be addressed when the case resolves.

Medicare Has Special Rules

If you have Medicare, pay close attention. Medicare has its own rules about injury claims, and the consequences for not following them can be serious.

Medicare is entitled to be repaid from your settlement or judgment for any injury-related treatment they covered. This is federal law, and it's strictly enforced.

Medicare may also require a "set-aside"—money from your settlement that gets reserved for future injury-related medical treatment.

The rules around Medicare set-asides are complex and depend on the specifics of your case.

If you have Medicare, give your attorney a copy of your Medicare card early. They need to report the claim to Medicare, track conditional payments, and make sure everything is handled in compliance with federal requirements. This is not optional.

Chapter 17 covers Medicare in more detail.

Medicaid in New Mexico

In New Mexico, Medicaid is administered through private insurance carriers who receive funding from the government. From your perspective as a patient, it functions similarly to marketplace or employer-provided health insurance.

That includes subrogation. If Medicaid pays for your injury-related treatment, they have the same right to reimbursement from your settlement that a private health insurer would have.

The discussion of subrogation above generally applies to Medicaid as well. Let your attorney know if you have Medicaid coverage so they can handle it appropriately.

Medicare Advantage Plans

If you're on a Medicare Advantage plan—a private plan that provides your Medicare benefits—your attorney needs to know. Medicare Advantage plans can have different rules and requirements that affect how your case is handled.

Don't assume your attorney will know what coverage you have. Tell them, and provide documentation.

Don't Ignore Your Bills

While your case is pending, don't simply ignore medical bills that arrive. Unpaid bills can go to collections, and that can affect your credit—even though you're expecting a settlement that will eventually cover them.

New Mexico has enacted some protections around medical debt collection and reporting. Laws like the Surprise Billing Act have changed some of the rules around how medical debt is handled. The details are beyond the scope of this book, but the protections exist.

If you receive a collection notice for injury-related medical bills, let your attorney know. There may be steps they can take, or information they can provide to the collector, to address the situation while your case is pending.

The important thing is not to just throw the notices away and hope for the best. Stay on top of it and keep your attorney informed.

This Is Technical—Let Your Attorney Handle It

The interplay between medical bills, health insurance payments, and subrogation claims is more complicated than it might seem.

Here's an example of the complexity. For any given treatment, there are usually three numbers: the amount the provider charged, the amount the health insurance company paid (after contractual adjustments), and the amount the health insurer claims they're entitled to in subrogation. These are often all different.

Sorting this out requires gathering specific records—explanation of benefits statements, billing records, payment histories. Then there's an opportunity to negotiate reductions in subrogation claims, which can put more money in your pocket.

This is something attorneys handle routinely, sometimes working with specialized vendors who focus on subrogation resolution. It's also something that people who handle claims on their own can easily miss or mishandle.

If you're working with an attorney, let them manage this. If you're handling your claim yourself, understand that this is one of the areas where professional help adds real value.

The Bottom Line

Medical bills don't wait for your case to settle. You need a plan for handling them in the meantime.

Use your health insurance if you have it. Understand that subrogation means some of your settlement will go back to your insurer. Don't ignore bills that arrive—keep your attorney informed so problems can be addressed.

This is one of the more technical aspects of an injury claim. Having professional help makes a real difference in getting it right.

CHAPTER 15

WHAT YOUR CASE IS WORTH

Everyone wants to know what their case is worth. It's the first question most people ask, and it's completely understandable. You've been hurt. You're dealing with medical bills, lost wages, pain, and disruption to your life. You want to know what you can expect.

Here's the honest answer: your case is worth whatever a jury will award for it.

That's true, but it's not particularly helpful. So let's dig deeper into how case valuation actually works.

The Categories of Damages

New Mexico law allows injured people to recover damages in several categories. These come from the jury instructions that govern trials, but they also guide how attorneys and insurance companies evaluate cases at every stage.

Compensatory damages are meant to compensate you for what you lost. They include:

- **Past and future medical expenses.** What you've already spent on treatment and what you'll need to spend going forward.
- **Past and future non-medical expenses caused by the injury.** Out-of-pocket costs like transportation to medical appointments, home modifications, or equipment you needed because of your injuries.
- **Past and future pain and suffering.** The physical pain you've experienced and will continue to experience.
- **Past and future loss of enjoyment of life.** The activities, hobbies, and pleasures you can no longer participate in because of your injuries.
- **The nature of the injury, including disfigurement.** Scarring, amputation, or other permanent changes to your body.
- **Lost income or wages.** Money you didn't earn because you couldn't work.
- **Loss of future earning potential.** If your injuries affect your ability to earn money going forward, that diminished capacity is compensable.
- **Loss of household services.** If you can't do chores around the house that you used to do, that has value too.

Additionally, spouses and children may have related claims for loss of consortium—damages to the relationship caused by your injuries.

Punitive damages are different. They're not meant to compensate you. They're meant to punish the at-fault party for particularly bad conduct. Punitive damages may be available when there was reckless, malicious, wanton, or willful behavior. In the premises context, this might involve a property owner who knew about a serious hazard, received multiple complaints, and deliberately chose to do nothing—prioritizing cost savings over safety.

Objective and Subjective Damages

Some of these damage categories are objective. They can be documented and calculated.

Medical expenses are based on what was billed in the past and what a medical expert will say is reasonably necessary in the future. Out-of-pocket expenses are shown by receipts and invoices. Past lost wages are documented through paystubs showing missed work and your typical wage or salary. Household services are typically valued at a modest hourly rate multiplied by the time you couldn't perform them.

These numbers can be pinned down through documentation.

Other categories are more subjective. Pain and suffering, loss of enjoyment of life, and damages for the nature of your injury or disfigurement—these are harder to quantify. They're about telling the story of how your injuries have affected your life.

Photographs help. Medical records documenting your condition help. Statements from family and friends who can describe the changes they've witnessed help. The goal is to paint a picture that a jury can understand and connect with.

A word of caution: decision-makers—judges and juries—don't like complainers or people who appear to be milking their case. Be honest and be reasonable. Exaggeration backfires.

The Reference Point Problem

Because the subjective damages are hard to pin down, everyone tends to evaluate them relative to the objective measures. Medical costs become the reference point.

This isn't right for every case. Sometimes people suffer enormously even with relatively low medical bills. A person with chronic pain who manages it through lifestyle changes rather than expensive procedures has still suffered. But in those cases, the qualitative evidence must be especially compelling.

If your medical bills are modest but your suffering is significant, you'll need to work harder to document and communicate the impact on your life.

Similar Cases Matter

The final ingredient in valuation is looking at settlements and verdicts from similar cases.

What have juries awarded for comparable injuries? What have similar cases settled for? This information helps establish a reasonable range.

Your attorney should have experience with similar cases and access to verdict and settlement databases. They may also consult with other attorneys to gut-check their own valuations—without revealing confidential information about your case.

The key is taking all this information—the documented damages, the subjective impacts, the comparable outcomes—and compiling it into a reasonable narrative that points to a reasonable range of values.

How Liability Affects Value in Premises Cases

Here's something specific to slip, trip, and fall cases: contested liability significantly affects valuation.

As we discussed in Chapter 2, premises cases almost always involve arguments about comparative fault. The defense will say you should have been watching where you were going, should have seen the hazard, should have avoided it. Juries are often receptive to these arguments.

This affects what your case is worth. Even if you have significant injuries and substantial medical bills, if there's a reasonable chance a jury will assign 30%, 40%, or 50% of the fault to you, that reduces the realistic value of your claim proportionally.

Your attorney factors this into their evaluation. A case with clear liability is worth more than an identical case where fault is contested—because the likelihood of full recovery is higher.

The Jury Perception Challenge

Another factor specific to premises cases: as we discussed in Chapter 2, juries don't intuitively understand how falls cause serious injuries.

A car crash involves obvious violence. Two vehicles colliding at speed—everyone understands how that could hurt someone badly. A fall seems less dramatic. Jurors may think: I've fallen before, and I was fine. How could this person be so badly injured?

This skepticism affects case values. Your attorney has to account for the possibility that a jury won't fully appreciate the severity of your injuries, even with strong medical documentation.

Cases with visible injuries—broken bones, surgeries, hardware implantation—tend to fare better because the harm is concrete and undeniable. Soft tissue injuries, chronic pain, and other conditions that don't show up on an X-ray face an uphill battle with juries.

The Biggest Misconception

The biggest misconception about case value is that people think their case is worth much more than it is.

The cases that make the news do so because they're rare, unusual, and noteworthy. And often, the severity of the injuries isn't fully reported. What you read in the headlines is often misinformation. The true facts of these cases are very different from what gets covered in the media.

Here's reality. Death, paralysis, around-the-clock home care, traumatic brain injuries resulting in severe impairment, inability to walk, or inability to work—these are the injuries that result in large verdicts or settlements.

If you haven't suffered something like this, be grateful that your injuries were not worse. And adjust your expectations accordingly.

The Insurance Reality

Here's another reality that limits case value: your potential recovery is usually capped at the amount of available insurance.

Sometimes that's not true. When the at-fault party is a business with significant assets beyond their insurance coverage, there may be more to recover. But pursuing assets beyond insurance is complicated and often not practical.

In the overwhelming majority of cases, the insurance is the maximum. If the available coverage is $100,000, that's the ceiling—no matter how badly you were injured.

The good news for premises cases, as we discussed earlier, is that commercial liability policies typically have higher limits than the minimum auto insurance policies many drivers carry. A typical commercial general liability policy provides $1 million in coverage, and some businesses carry excess policies on top of that.

But the principle remains: available insurance usually sets the ceiling on recovery. This is why your attorney works early in the case to identify all responsible parties and all available coverage.

What You Can Do to Help

Outside of catastrophic cases, the best thing you can do to help establish the true value of your case is to help gather the information your attorney needs to tell a compelling story.

Get your attorney in touch with family members and friends who can validate changes in your lifestyle. Help them understand who you were before the fall and who you are now.

Talk about hobbies you used to enjoy but can't anymore. Describe activities that are now difficult or impossible. Document how your daily life has changed.

Your attorney can compile the medical records and bills. But you're the one who can bring the human story to life.

Demand vs. Valuation

One thing people should understand: the first number we put forward—the demand—is not the valuation of your case.

The demand is a high figure that gives us room to negotiate. If I suggest an initial demand of $100,000, that means I think a fair settlement for the case is likely somewhere between $40,000 and $60,000.

The insurance company will respond with a low number—maybe $10,000. Then we negotiate from there, each side moving toward a reasonable compromise.

Don't confuse the demand with what your case is worth. The demand is a negotiating position.

Why Pushing Longer Can Increase Offers

Generally, the longer we stay in the fight, the more the insurance company will offer. There are two reasons for this.

First, time in litigation clarifies the facts. As we take depositions, gather evidence, and work up the case, everyone learns more about what actually happened and what a trial might look like. The perceived range of possible outcomes narrows. That pushes both sides toward compromise.

Second, litigation costs money. As the case goes on, both sides incur attorney fees and case costs—especially expert witness fees. At some point, the cost of continuing to fight tips the balance toward offering a reasonable settlement.

Diminishing Returns

That said, there's a point of diminishing returns.

Sometimes we reach a crossroads where the conversation with the client looks like this: the insurance company has offered X. The next stage in litigation is to hire expert witnesses—maybe multiple experts—to make our case at trial. That's going to cost Y.

Good testimony from our experts might increase their offer. But if the increase is approximately Y, what have we gained? We've spent the additional money just to end up in roughly the same place.

These are judgment calls. They depend on the specific facts of your case, the amount at stake, and your own appetite for continued litigation.

The Fundamental Uncertainty

Here's the most important thing to understand about case valuation: we don't know.

We simply don't know what might happen at trial. We don't know what a jury—twelve people chosen essentially at random from the public—might think about your case and your injuries.

Think about the makeup of a jury. Jury selection isn't really "picking a jury." We don't get to decide who decides your case. Jury selection is really about identifying and keeping extremists off the panel. What you end up with is twelve essentially unremarkable people.

They could be very liberal or very conservative. Someone might philosophically oppose large damage awards. Someone else might have fallen and gotten nothing, making them skeptical of injury claims. Another might have never dealt with insurance and have no perspective. They could be eighteen years old or eighty. Scientists or high school dropouts.

This uncertainty is irreducible. No one can tell you exactly what a jury will do.

What You're Left With

For the majority of cases, you're working from your attorney's background experience and their consultations with other attorneys who handle similar matters.

It's not a crystal ball. It's informed judgment based on years of handling cases, knowledge of what similar situations have settled for, and an understanding of how juries in New Mexico tend to respond.

Your attorney should be able to give you a reasonable range. But understand that it's a range, not a guarantee. The uncertainty is built into the system.

The Bottom Line

Your case is worth what a jury would award—minus whatever fault they assign to you. But since we can't know exactly what a jury will do, valuation is informed estimation based on the documented damages, the strength of liability, comparable cases, and the available insurance.

Work with your attorney to tell a compelling story about how your injuries have affected your life. Understand the demand is a negotiating position, not a prediction. And keep your expectations grounded in reality, not headlines.

CHAPTER 16

NEGOTIATING A SETTLEMENT

Most premises liability cases settle. They don't go to trial. They don't result in a dramatic verdict. Instead, sometime in the process, the two sides reach an agreement, paperwork gets signed, and a check arrives.

Understanding how settlement negotiation works helps you participate meaningfully in the process and set realistic expectations about what's happening and why.

Pre-Litigation Negotiation

Before a lawsuit is filed, you're typically dealing with a liability adjuster at the insurance company. That adjuster is often located out of state, handling hundreds of files simultaneously.

Insurance companies don't evaluate cases the way you might expect. They use tools and algorithms—proprietary databases, either built in-house or licensed from third-party companies. The adjuster inputs certain information, like liability assessments and medical treatment codes, and the system generates a "value" for the case.

This process is impersonal. It doesn't account for qualitative factors—how your injuries have actually affected your life, the specific circumstances of your fall, the story behind the numbers. The data the system relies on may be imperfect or biased.

This is what asymmetry looks like. Insurance companies have spent decades and billions of dollars building systems to process claims efficiently—which, from their perspective, means paying less. You're bringing a pen to what is increasingly a data fight.

The adjuster on the other end of the phone isn't your adversary in the way you might think. They're a person doing a difficult job inside a system designed to constrain them. They're monitored, measured on metrics, and juggling more files than any one person can meaningfully manage. The algorithm suggests a number. The adjuster's job is to defend it.

This matters for how you think about negotiation. If the person across the table has limited authority to deviate from what the system says, human-to-human persuasion only goes so far. Moving the needle often requires action—usually litigation—that changes the inputs the system is weighing. It's not about convincing the adjuster. It's about changing the calculus.

In terms of pure mechanics, pre-litigation negotiation is straightforward. Your attorney makes a demand. The insurance company responds with an offer. Then it's back and forth—counter-offers until you either reach a resolution or decide you're not making progress.

The Liability Challenge in Premises Negotiations

Here's something specific to slip, trip, and fall cases: insurance companies are often more aggressive in pre-litigation negotiations because they believe liability is contestable.

As we've discussed throughout this book, the defense in premises cases almost always argues comparative fault. They'll claim you should have seen the hazard, should have been watching where you walked, should have worn different shoes. These arguments have traction with juries, and insurance companies know it.

This affects negotiation. An adjuster handling a car accident case where their insured ran a red light knows liability is clear. They're mainly negotiating over damages. An adjuster handling a slip and fall case may genuinely believe—or at least argue—that liability is uncertain. They'll use that uncertainty to justify lower offers.

Your attorney counters this by building a strong case on liability: evidence of the hazard, documentation that the property owner knew or should have known about it, expert opinions on what reasonable care required. The stronger your liability case, the less room the insurance company has to hide behind comparative fault arguments.

The Only Real Leverage

If pre-litigation negotiation stalls, the only real leverage your attorney has is to sue.

Filing a lawsuit changes the dynamic. It signals that you're serious about pursuing the case. It starts a clock running. It creates costs and pressures that didn't exist before.

But here's something important to understand: a lawsuit does not equal a trial.

When your attorney files a lawsuit—initiated by a document called a complaint that causes the court to open an official record with a case number—trial could still be years away. There are many opportunities to reach a settlement between filing suit and actually walking into a courtroom.

Filing a lawsuit is a step in the process, not the end of the process.

How Litigation Changes Negotiation

Once a lawsuit is filed, negotiations look different.

You're typically no longer dealing with the same out-of-state adjuster who handled the pre-litigation file. Now there's a local defense attorney on the other side—someone hired by the insurance company to represent their insured. That attorney reports to an adjuster, often a different one than before.

Defense costs for the insurance company start accruing immediately. The defense attorney gets paid by the hour. Every motion, every deposition, every piece of discovery costs the insurance company money.

You also gain access to evidence through the discovery process. You can take depositions—sworn testimony from witnesses, property managers, maintenance workers, even corporate representatives. Information that was hidden before becomes available. In premises cases, this is particularly valuable because you can finally obtain internal documents like maintenance logs, inspection records, and prior incident reports.

The court may order the parties to attend mediation—a structured settlement conference designed to encourage resolution.

The fundamental mechanics remain the same: offers and counter-offers. But the pressures on the insurance company have escalated significantly.

What Mediation Looks Like

Mediation is a settlement process that typically happens over a day or half a day. A neutral third party—the mediator—acts as an intermediary between the two sides, trying to facilitate an agreement.

Mediators are often retired judges who bring real courtroom experience to the table. They've seen thousands of cases. They can offer feedback and reality checks to both sides based on what they've witnessed over their careers.

Here's how it works. Everyone gathers—the attorneys, their clients, and insurance representatives. But the two sides don't sit in the same room negotiating face to face. Instead, each side goes to a separate room. These might be physical conference rooms in the same building, or they might be virtual rooms on a video call.

The mediator moves back and forth between the rooms, carrying information and offers. They'll share what the other side is proposing, provide their own assessment of the strengths and weaknesses of each position, and try to guide both parties toward a middle ground.

The advantage of mediation is speed. Offers and counter-offers happen within minutes or hours rather than days or weeks. A negotiation that might have taken months through letters and phone calls can potentially be resolved in a single day.

Mediation doesn't always result in settlement. But it often does, and even when it doesn't, it usually moves the parties closer together.

Evaluating Whether an Offer Is Reasonable

When a settlement offer comes in, how do you know if it's fair?

I advise clients based on the factors we discussed in the previous chapter. The best guidance I can give is whether I believe the offer is fair compared to similar cases. What have other people with comparable injuries received? How does this offer stack up?

In premises cases, I also factor in the liability risk. If there's a meaningful chance a jury will assign significant fault to you, that affects what constitutes a fair offer. A case with contested liability might reasonably settle for less than an identical case where fault is clear—because the expected value at trial is lower.

More than anything, I want my clients to receive a fair shake. I don't want to help people milk a case inappropriately—that's not who I am. But I also don't want them to be undercompensated for real injuries and real losses.

Different attorneys have different philosophies. Some care most about resolving cases quickly and handling a large volume. Some want to push every case as hard as possible, hoping to maximize recovery. That second approach sounds appealing, but it increases costs and increases risks.

I care most about fairness. If I feel like I got my client a fair result—in the mix with other people in similar situations—I rest easy with the job I did.

The Easy Versus Hard Framework

Here's how I often explain settlement offers to clients.

The other side—the insurance company—can make things easy or make things hard.

They make things easy by offering a lowball number. A clearly inadequate offer is easy to reject. You don't have to agonize over it. The answer is obviously no, and we keep negotiating or move toward litigation.

They also make things easy by offering a high figure—typically at or near the policy limits when there's a coverage cap. A near-maximum offer is easy to accept. You know you're getting most of what's available, and saying yes is straightforward.

They make things hard by offering a number in the middle. A middle-ground offer creates conflicting feelings. You wonder if you could do better. You also fear you could do worse. You're not sure whether to accept, reject, or counter.

If you're experiencing those conflicting feelings—simultaneously pulled toward yes and toward no—it probably means you're in the neighborhood of a true compromise position. Neither side is thrilled, but neither side is being treated unfairly.

Your attorney can offer guidance, but ultimately this is the client's decision to make.

It's Not Just About the Money

Settlement decisions aren't purely about case value. They're also about your goals and your risk tolerance.

Some clients just want to close this chapter of their lives. They're tired of dealing with the fall, the insurance company, the legal process. Getting a fair offer and moving on has real value to them, even if pushing harder might yield a bit more money.

Some clients want their day in court. They want to tell their story to a jury. They want accountability. They're willing to accept the risk of a bad result for the chance at vindication.

Most clients fall somewhere in between. They just want to know they've been treated fairly.

There's no single right answer. The right settlement depends on who you are and what matters to you.

Negotiations Can Always Restart

Settlement talks can stall. You might reach an impasse where neither side is willing to move. It can feel like the negotiation is over.

But negotiations can almost always restart. Negotiations are not concluded until you have signed a settlement agreement or the case has been fully litigated to conclusion, including all appeals and all collection efforts.

Even during trial, the parties can negotiate. Even after a verdict, while an appeal is pending, settlement discussions can happen. The case isn't truly over until it's over.

What changes is the context. Events during litigation—depositions that go well or poorly, rulings from the judge, the approach of a trial date—influence the range of values that both sides are willing to consider. A settlement that wasn't possible six months ago might become possible after new information emerges.

Keep this in mind if negotiations seem to have hit a wall. The wall might not be permanent.

Common Mistakes in Negotiation

People make predictable mistakes during settlement negotiations that can hurt their outcomes.

Rushing to the bottom line. Some people want to skip the back-and-forth and just get to the final number. This isn't how attorneys and insurance companies approach negotiation. If you rush to your bottom line, the other side will simply negotiate against that number—treating it as your opening position rather than your final offer. You end up with less than you should have gotten.

Thinking of it like buying a car. When you negotiate for a car, you know you can walk away and go to a different dealership if talks break down. That knowledge gives you leverage.

Injury claims don't work that way. There's no other insurance company to go to. If you're going to get any money, it's coming from the responsible parties' insurance coverage. You're stuck with these parties.

Understand the dynamic you're in, not the one you're used to from other contexts.

It's a Process

The most important thing to understand about settlement negotiation is that it's a process.

The first offer tells you basically nothing. It's a starting position, not a serious assessment of your case's value. After several rounds of back and forth, a clearer picture emerges of how the other side is actually valuing the case and what compromise might be possible.

It's also important to try to understand why the insurance company is doing what they're doing.

Their evaluation process is opaque. It's subject to pressures and incentives that may have nothing to do with your specific case—things like quarterly targets, adjuster caseloads, or corporate policies about certain types of claims. But it's not irrational.

When the insurance company takes a position that seems unfair or unreasonable, they may be responding to a perceived or actual weakness in your case. Maybe there's a gap in your treatment history. Maybe liability isn't as clear as you think. Maybe something in your medical records raised a red flag. In premises cases especially, they may be banking on comparative fault arguments that they believe will resonate with a jury.

You want to understand what's driving their position so you can either address it head-on or adjust your own expectations accordingly.

Throughout the process, keep the statute of limitations in mind. In New Mexico, most injury claims must be filed within three years. But remember: if your fall occurred on government property, the Tort Claims Act imposes much shorter deadlines—including a 90-day notice requirement. Negotiations can stretch on, but critical deadlines don't wait. Your attorney should be tracking this, but you should know about it too.

The Bottom Line

Settlement negotiation is a process, not an event. It involves offers and counter-offers, strategic decisions about when to push harder and when to accept a fair compromise, and ultimately a judgment call about what resolution meets your goals.

Work with your attorney to understand where you stand, what a fair outcome looks like, and what risks you're willing to accept. The right settlement is the one that treats you fairly and lets you move forward with your life.

CHAPTER 17

SPECIAL RULES FOR MEDICARE RECIPIENTS

If you're on Medicare, your injury claim involves additional rules and requirements that don't apply to people with private health insurance. These rules come from federal law, and the consequences for getting them wrong can be serious.

This chapter explains what Medicare recipients need to know and why working closely with your attorney on these issues is essential.

Why Medicare Is Different

When Medicare pays for medical treatment related to your fall, federal law says they have a right to be paid back.

This comes from the Medicare Secondary Payer Recovery Act. The principle is straightforward: if Medicare paid for your injuries and a different entity should have paid—like the property owner's liability insurance—then Medicare can recover what they spent from any settlement or judgment you receive.

So far, this sounds similar to the subrogation claims we discussed in Chapter 14 with private health insurance. In Medicare terminology, these payments are called Medicare conditional payments. And like other subrogation claims, conditional payment amounts can often be negotiated down.

But that's where the similarities end. Medicare has rules that go beyond what private insurers can do, and the stakes for non-compliance are much higher.

Consequence for Non-Compliance: Losing Eligibility

Here's the most serious difference. If Medicare's conditional payment claim is not properly resolved, you could lose your Medicare eligibility.

That's not a typo. Failing to address Medicare's recovery rights can result in losing your health coverage.

This is why it's imperative that Medicare conditional payments be addressed in every case involving a Medicare recipient. It's not optional. It's not something to deal with later. Your attorney needs to handle this, and you need to make sure it's happening.

Medicare Set-Asides: Protecting Future Treatment

Unlike private health insurers, Medicare's right to reimbursement doesn't necessarily end when your claim ends.

If your settlement involves the potential for future medical treatment related to your fall, Medicare's interests may need to be taken into account. This means that some portion of your settlement might need to be set aside to pay for future fall-related care before Medicare starts covering those expenses again.

This is called a Medicare set-aside.

The law in this area is not entirely clear. There are ongoing legal debates, and guidance from CMS—the Centers for Medicare and Medicaid Services—has been murky. But the requirement appears to exist, and ignoring it creates risk.

How much needs to be set aside? That depends on your specific situation—what future treatment you're likely to need, what it will cost, and actuarial calculations about timing and life expectancy.

This is not something you or your attorney should try to figure out on your own.

Using Expert Vendors for Set-Aside Analysis

There are companies that specialize in Medicare set-aside planning. They employ experts who analyze your treatment needs, review medical records, research costs, apply actuarial data, and produce a formal plan that calculates an appropriate set-aside amount in current dollars.

If your case needs a Medicare set-aside due to expected future treatment, one of these vendors should be engaged. This is specialized work that requires specialized expertise.

The cost of a set-aside analysis varies, and not every case justifies the expense. A small settlement might not warrant spending thousands of dollars on expert analysis. But for cases with significant future treatment needs, it's an essential step.

When Is a Set-Aside Necessary?

This is where things get frustrating. The official guidance on when a Medicare set-aside is required in liability cases is unclear.

Some attorneys believe, based on certain federal memos, that set-asides are never required in liability cases—only in workers' compensation cases. In my opinion, that interpretation is too risky. The potential consequences of getting this wrong are too serious to rely on an aggressive reading of ambiguous guidance.

My approach: it's best practice to recommend a set-aside analysis whenever there's a reasonable probability that you'll need future medical care related to your fall injuries. Better to address it deliberately than to discover years later that you should have.

What the Process Looks Like

Your attorney should contact Medicare early in your case to get information about conditional payments—what Medicare has paid so far for your fall-related treatment.

One important note: Medicare does not review or approve set-asides in liability cases. Unlike workers' compensation cases, where you can submit a set-aside proposal to CMS for approval, there's no such process for liability claims. You're making your best judgment based on expert analysis, not getting a government stamp of approval.

This is another reason why working with experienced vendors and attorneys matters. You're navigating uncertain territory, and you need people who understand the landscape.

What You Need to Provide

From your end, the most important thing is simple: give your attorney your Medicare ID and number at the outset of your case.

Your attorney should take it from there—contacting Medicare, tracking conditional payments, determining whether a set-aside analysis is appropriate, and engaging vendors if needed.

But it starts with you providing that basic information. If you're on Medicare, tell your attorney immediately and provide your Medicare card.

The Client's Decision

Ultimately, whether to pay for a Medicare set-aside analysis is your decision.

Not every recovery justifies the cost. If your settlement is modest and future treatment needs are minimal or speculative, spending several thousand dollars on a formal set-aside analysis might not make sense.

But the choice should be made deliberately, in discussion with your attorney. You need to understand the risks of not doing a set-aside, weigh them against the costs of doing one, and make an informed decision.

Don't let this issue slide by without consideration. Address it one way or another.

Medicare Eligibility Can Arise Mid-Case

Here's something that surprises people: Medicare issues can come up even if you weren't on Medicare at the time of your fall.

If you become eligible for Medicare while your case is pending, these rules start to apply. If you're going to become eligible in the next couple of years—because you're approaching age sixty-five or because of a disability determination—that can affect how your settlement needs to be structured.

This is another reason to keep your attorney informed about changes in your situation. If your Medicare status changes, or is about to change, your attorney needs to know.

The Bottom Line

Medicare adds a layer of complexity to injury claims that private health insurance doesn't. The stakes are higher—including the potential loss of Medicare eligibility—and the rules around set-asides are uncertain enough to require careful, deliberate attention.

If you're on Medicare, or expect to become eligible during your case, make sure your attorney knows from the start. Provide your Medicare card. Ask about how conditional payments are being tracked. Discuss whether a set-aside analysis makes sense for your situation.

This is technical, specialized territory. It's exactly the kind of issue where professional help makes a real difference.

CHAPTER 18

WHEN YOUR CASE GOES TO COURT

This chapter provides a high-level overview of the litigation process. It's meant to prepare you for discussions with your attorney, not to serve as a comprehensive guide.

Litigation involves many ins and outs that go beyond what any single chapter can cover—special rules about handling medical records, ways that case costs can increase or be shifted between parties, details about witness presentation, procedures for handling subpoenas, and much more. Your attorney should go in-depth on the things that matter for your specific case.

Sometimes a lawsuit gets filed because the statute of limitations is approaching. In New Mexico, most injury claims must be filed within three years. If negotiations are still ongoing as that deadline nears, your attorney will file suit to preserve the claim—even if both sides expect to keep negotiating toward a settlement.

Remember, as we discussed in Chapter 11, if your fall occurred on government property, the deadlines are much shorter. The Tort Claims Act requires notice within 90 days, and the timeline for filing suit is compressed. Your attorney should be tracking these deadlines carefully.

What follows is a preview of what to expect if your case moves from negotiation into the court system.

Litigation Does Not Mean Trial

The most important thing to understand: filing a lawsuit does not mean you're going to trial.

Litigation means filing a lawsuit and getting a case opened in the court system. That starts a process that could lead to trial—but most cases don't get there. The overwhelming majority settle somewhere along the way.

It's best to think of litigation as the next stage in the negotiation process. Filing suit increases pressure on the insurance company. It creates costs for them. It moves toward a resolution with a deadline attached. But it doesn't commit you to seeing the case through to a jury verdict.

Settlement can occur at any time during litigation—even during trial itself.

The Stages of Litigation

Once a lawsuit is filed, the case moves through several stages.

Discovery. Discovery is the formal process through which the parties to a case are required to make certain information available to each other. This typically happens in three ways.

Written discovery requests, officially called interrogatories, require you to answer questions in writing and under oath. The other side will ask about the fall, your injuries, your treatment, your work history, and other relevant topics. Your attorney will help you prepare your responses.

Document sharing, officially called requests for production, requires you to provide documentation. This might include medical records, employment records, photographs, or other materials relevant to your case.

Depositions are formal questioning sessions. Parties and witnesses may be required to answer questions while a court reporter creates a transcript. Depositions can also be video recorded. Your attorney will prepare you before your deposition and be present during it.

In premises cases, discovery is particularly valuable because it's often the first opportunity to obtain the property owner's internal documents—maintenance logs, inspection records, incident reports, employee communications, and similar materials that were unavailable before litigation.

In some cases, physical examinations may be required. When someone claims injuries, they typically support those claims through testimony from their own medical experts. The other side may request that their expert witnesses be allowed to conduct an independent medical examination of the claimant. If this happens in your case, your attorney will explain what to expect.

Mediation. During or after discovery, the court will typically order the parties to participate in mediation. We discussed mediation in the previous chapter—a settlement conference with a neutral facilitator trying to help both sides reach agreement.

Trial. At some point, typically at the parties' request, the judge will schedule a trial date. If the case doesn't settle before then, the trial happens and a judge or jury makes a decision.

A great deal of preparation goes into trial—witness lists, exhibit preparation, jury selection, opening statements, examination of witnesses, closing arguments. The details are beyond the scope of this book. Your attorney will work with you extensively to prepare if your case reaches this stage.

Appeal. After trial, the side that loses has the opportunity to appeal. This means asking the New Mexico Court of Appeals to review the legal decisions made by the trial judge to determine whether they were in accordance with New Mexico law.

If the appeals court finds an error, they may return the case to the trial court for a new trial. If they find no error, they "affirm" the judgment—upholding the trial court's decision and ordering it to be enforced.

Each of these stages could fill a book of its own. What matters for now is understanding the general sequence and knowing that your attorney will guide you through the specifics.

How Long Does Litigation Take?

A typical injury case in New Mexico may go to trial somewhere between one and three years after the filing of the lawsuit. This is measured from when the lawsuit is filed, not from the date of the fall.

If there's an appeal after trial, add several more years.

These timelines vary based on the complexity of the case, the court's schedule, and how aggressively both sides pursue or delay proceedings. Your attorney can give you a better estimate based on the specifics of your situation and which court your case is in.

Remember: settlement can happen at any point along this timeline, and most cases do settle before trial.

A Note on Bernalillo County

In Bernalillo County, certain claims—generally those where the claimant is seeking less than $50,000—must participate in mandatory arbitration. This is a court-ordered process that functions differently from a traditional trial.

If your case is filed in Bernalillo County and this applies to you, your attorney will explain what mandatory arbitration means and how it relates to the other stages of litigation.

What Litigation Feels Like for Clients

For clients, litigation is mostly waiting.

The case trudges forward through procedural stages, most of which happen without your direct involvement. Attorneys file motions. Documents get exchanged. Deadlines come and go. You might not hear much for weeks at a time.

That waiting is punctuated by a few occasions where you personally have to be involved—usually in stressful ways. The main client involvement points are:

- **Answering written discovery.** You'll need to respond to interrogatories and help gather documents.
- **Sitting for a deposition.** You'll be questioned under oath by the other side's attorney while a court reporter transcribes everything.
- **Participating in mediation.** You'll attend the settlement conference, either in person or virtually, and be involved in decisions about offers and counteroffers.
- **Testifying at trial.** If your case goes that far, you'll tell your story to the judge or jury.

Depositions Are Often the Most Stressful

Clients who have gone through all these stages often tell me that sitting for a deposition was the most stressful part.

That might seem counterintuitive. You'd think trial would be the hardest—the stakes are highest, the courtroom is formal, there's a jury watching. But for many clients, trial brings a sense of relief. It's finally their chance to tell their story in open court. It's the "day in court" they've been waiting for.

A deposition is different. You're being questioned by the opposing attorney, whose job is to find weaknesses in your case. There's no jury to appeal to. It can feel like an interrogation.

In premises cases, expect questions about everything we've discussed throughout this book: what you were doing when you fell, what shoes you were wearing, whether you saw the hazard, whether you were distracted, your medical history, prior falls, and more. The defense attorney will be looking for anything that supports a comparative fault argument.

Your attorney will work with you closely to prepare for your deposition. They'll explain what to expect, go over likely questions, and help you understand how to respond. You won't go in blind.

The same applies if you're required to undergo a physical examination by the other side's medical expert. Your attorney will prepare you for what that involves.

If You Lose at Trial

Going to trial means accepting the possibility of losing. If the jury doesn't rule in your favor, there can be significant consequences.

You'll likely still have to reimburse your attorney for case costs—the expenses that were advanced during litigation. Depending on the circumstances, you might also be liable for some of the other party's costs.

Before you decide to reject a settlement offer and proceed to trial, have a realistic discussion with your attorney about these possibilities. Understand what you're risking, not just what you might gain.

Appeals Are Uphill Battles

If you lose at trial, you have the right to appeal. But it's important to understand that most appeals are unsuccessful. The losing side faces an uphill battle.

The reason is that trial courts—as the courts presiding over the actual trial, hearing live testimony, and observing witnesses—are given substantial deference on many legal issues. The appeals court isn't going to second-guess every decision the trial judge made. They're looking for significant legal errors, and those don't occur in most cases.

Something else that surprises people: appeals don't involve new testimony or new evidence. The appeals court reviews the record that was created at the trial court level—the filings, documents, evidence, and transcripts. You don't get to present your case again. You're arguing that legal mistakes were made the first time.

The Biggest Misconception

The biggest misconception about litigation is that filing a lawsuit definitely means going to trial and getting a decision from a judge or jury.

It doesn't. Filing a lawsuit starts a lengthy process that could end in trial, but most cases settle along the way. The filing itself, the discovery process, the approach of a trial date—all of these create pressure that often leads to resolution.

Think of litigation as another stage in negotiation, one with higher stakes and greater pressure on both sides. The possibility of trial focuses everyone's attention. But the goal, in most cases, remains finding a fair settlement.

The Bottom Line

Litigation is a process, not a destination. Filing a lawsuit doesn't mean you're going to trial—it means you're entering a stage where settlement becomes more likely because the pressure on both sides has increased.

If your case does go to litigation, expect a timeline measured in years, not months. Your direct involvement will be limited to a few key moments: answering discovery, sitting for a deposition, participating in mediation, and potentially testifying at trial.

Your attorney will guide you through each step. The process is stressful, but it's manageable—and for many cases, it's the path to a fair resolution that wouldn't have been possible through negotiation alone.

CHAPTER 19

THE ROLE OF EXPERT WITNESSES

Expert witnesses can make or break a premises liability case. We've mentioned experts throughout this book—safety experts who establish that a condition was hazardous, medical experts who connect your injuries to your fall. This chapter explains their role in more detail and why they matter so much.

Why Experts Are Often Necessary

In many types of cases, the facts speak for themselves. A driver runs a red light and causes a collision. A jury doesn't need an expert to explain why that was negligent.

Premises cases are different. As we discussed in Chapter 8, what constitutes a hazard—and what constitutes reasonable care—depends heavily on context. Industry standards, common practices, the nature of the business, the specific circumstances of the property all factor in. These aren't things a typical juror knows intuitively.

That's where experts come in. They provide the specialized knowledge that helps a jury understand why the property owner's conduct was unreasonable and why your injuries are real and connected to your fall.

Medical Experts

Medical experts help establish that your treatment was reasonable, necessary, and caused by the incident.

This might seem straightforward—you fell, you were hurt, you got treatment. But the defense will challenge all of it. They'll argue your injuries predated the fall. They'll claim your treatment was excessive. They'll suggest your ongoing symptoms have nothing to do with what happened on their client's property.

Medical experts counter these arguments. A treating physician or an independent medical expert can explain the mechanism of injury, connect your condition to the fall, and establish that the treatment you received was appropriate.

Depending on the nature and severity of your injuries, multiple medical experts may be needed. A case involving back injuries, a head injury, and chronic pain might require specialists in each area. Each expert adds to the cost, but each may be necessary to tell the complete story of what happened to you.

Some cases also require specialized experts to address the cost of care. If you have significant future medical needs, an expert may be needed to calculate what that care will cost over your lifetime. In cases involving severe, life-altering injuries, a life care planner—an expert who develops comprehensive plans for ongoing care—may be necessary.

Safety Experts

Safety experts are often the key witnesses in premises cases. They establish two critical things: that a particular condition was unsafe (a hazard), and that the property owner's policies for inspection, maintenance, and response were unreasonable.

Remember what we discussed in Chapter 8: liability in these cases depends on context. What's reasonable for one type of business isn't reasonable for another. What's acceptable in one environment would be dangerous in another. Safety experts help illuminate what's reasonable in a given context based on general practices, industry standards, regulatory requirements, and their professional judgment.

Importantly, safety experts can explain why something that appears innocuous is actually a hazard. A slope in a sidewalk that's too steep. A misaligned edge measured in fractions of an inch. A floor coating that becomes dangerously slick when wet. These subtle conditions don't look dangerous to the average person—which is precisely why they're so hazardous. Pedestrians don't notice them. They don't adjust their gait or take extra care. And then they fall.

Safety experts help tell that story. They take measurements, review standards, analyze the property owner's practices, and explain to a jury why what looks like nothing was actually a serious problem that should have been addressed.

The Cost of Experts

Here's the difficult reality: experts are expensive.

Experts typically charge by the hour. By the time they've reviewed your case, inspected the scene, prepared a written report, testified at a deposition, and appeared at trial, the costs can be substantial. A fully litigated and tried premises case could involve tens of thousands of dollars in expert fees.

This is one of the biggest differences between premises cases and simpler injury claims. In a car accident case where someone ran a red light, you might need a medical expert but probably not much else. In a premises case with contested liability, you may need both medical and safety experts—and possibly multiple experts in each category.

The size of the case, the potential recovery, and the probability of recovery all have to justify the expense. Your attorney evaluates this carefully. If the potential recovery is modest and the liability is uncertain, spending $30,000 on experts doesn't make sense. If the injuries are serious and the case is strong, the investment may be essential to achieving a fair outcome.

Fee Shifting: The Risk of Losing

Under court rules, expert fees can sometimes be shifted between the parties. If you win, you may be able to have some of your expert fees paid by the defense as part of the judgment.

But the reverse is also true. If you lose at trial, you could be required to pay not only your own expert fees but also the defense's expert costs. The rule that makes the losing side pay case costs can include expert witness fees.

This creates real risk. Before you decide to reject a settlement offer and proceed to trial, understand what's at stake. If the trial doesn't go your way, you could end up responsible for significant costs on both sides.

The Defense Will Have Experts Too

Your experts won't be the only voices in the room. The defense will likely hire their own experts to contest the opinions of your experts.

A defense safety expert may argue that the condition wasn't actually hazardous, or that the property owner's practices were reasonable, or that you should have noticed and avoided the problem. A defense medical expert may argue that your injuries were pre-existing, that your treatment was excessive, or that your ongoing symptoms aren't related to the fall.

Expert testimony often becomes a battle of competing opinions. Each side presents experts who support their position. The jury decides who to believe.

This is why your attorney's choice of experts matters. Experts with strong credentials, clear communication skills, and credibility with juries make a difference. An expert who can explain complex concepts in plain language—who can help the jury see what they'd otherwise miss—is worth the investment.

When We Proceed Without a Safety Expert

Not every premises case requires a safety expert. Sometimes the liability is clear enough that a lay person can understand it without specialized help.

A large puddle of water in the middle of a grocery store aisle, captured in photographs, with evidence that it sat there for an hour before anyone cleaned it up—a jury can understand why that's negligent without an expert explaining it.

But these clear-cut cases are the exception, not the rule. In most contested premises cases, safety experts are necessary to establish what the standard of care required and how the property owner fell short.

Your attorney evaluates whether expert testimony is needed based on the specific facts of your case. If liability is genuinely obvious, proceeding without a safety expert saves significant costs. If there's any reasonable argument about whether the condition was hazardous or whether the property owner's practices were adequate, expert testimony is usually essential.

The Bottom Line

Expert witnesses add cost and complexity to premises cases. But in most contested cases, they're essential. Medical experts connect your injuries to your fall and establish that your treatment was appropriate. Safety experts establish that a hazard existed and that the property owner's conduct was unreasonable.

The expense is significant—potentially tens of thousands of dollars in a fully litigated case. That expense has to be justified by the size of the potential recovery and the strength of the case. And the risk of losing at trial includes the possibility of paying for experts on both sides.

Your attorney will guide you through these decisions. When experts are needed, they'll help you find the right ones. When the case can proceed without them, they'll explain why. Either way, you should understand the role experts play and why they matter so much in premises liability cases.

CHAPTER 20

CLOSING YOUR CASE AND GETTING PAID

You've reached a settlement. The number has been agreed upon. Now you want your money.

People often think they can get a check the next day, or at least within a week. That's not how it works. Several things need to happen between agreeing on a settlement and actually receiving your take-home amount. Understanding the process helps you know what to expect—and why it takes longer than you might think.

The Settlement Agreement

When the sides agree on a number, that's not the end. It's the beginning of the documentation process.

The attorneys draw up a settlement agreement—a legally binding contract that spells out all the terms of the deal. This isn't just a piece of paper with a dollar figure on it. At a minimum, a settlement agreement makes crystal clear that the responsible party and their insurance company are completely released from any further liability, that any pending litigation will be dismissed, and that the claimant will never seek more money from them.

That last point bears emphasis. Once you settle, you're done with that party. Forever. You cannot go back for more money, no matter what happens with your injuries down the road.

This is why timing matters. You need to be done with treatment, or have a clear understanding of what future treatment you'll need, or at least be making a deliberate decision with your eyes wide open. Settling too early—before you know the full extent of your injuries—can leave you with expenses that will never be covered.

It may take weeks for the attorneys to work out the details of the settlement agreement. Drafts get passed back and forth. Language gets negotiated. Terms get clarified. This is normal, but it takes time.

Signing and Execution

Once the settlement agreement is finalized, you'll need to sign it. This will likely require a notary to notarize your signature.

Your attorney will then provide the executed—meaning signed—agreement to the other side. It's usually at that point when the insurance company sends the settlement check.

Subrogation and Lien Negotiation

While waiting for the check, your attorney should be working on another piece of the puzzle.

If your health insurance paid for fall-related treatment, they have a subrogation claim—a right to be repaid from your settlement. If any medical providers filed liens against your case, those need to be resolved too.

Your attorney contacts these subrogated carriers and lienholders to negotiate reductions and get final numbers. As we discussed in Chapter 14, these amounts are often negotiable. But the negotiation takes time, and the final numbers need to be known before your attorney can tell you exactly what your take-home amount will be.

The Trust Account and Clearing Period

When the settlement check arrives, your attorney doesn't hand it straight to you. The check gets deposited into the attorney's trust account—a special account used to hold client funds.

Then there's a waiting period. Usually seven to ten business days to ensure the check clears.

This might seem overly cautious, but there's good reason for it. A careful attorney will not start disbursing funds quickly after receiving an insurance check. If the check bounces and the attorney has already written checks against it, the result is insufficient funds in the trust account. That causes serious problems—for you, for the attorney, and for the attorney's other clients whose funds are also held in that account.

Waiting for the check to clear is standard practice and protects everyone.

Final Disbursement

Even once the check clears, your attorney can't cut you a check until everything else is resolved.

The subrogation claims need to be finalized. The lien amounts need to be confirmed. All the numbers need to be known so the math works out correctly.

Once everything is in place, you'll receive a disbursement statement. This document spells out exactly what's coming out of your settlement and what your final take-home amount will be.

The math looks like this:

Total settlement amount, minus attorney fees, minus taxes on those fees (gross receipts tax, as we discussed in Chapter 6), minus reimbursement of case costs your attorney advanced, minus required payments to subrogated carriers or lienholders, equals your final take-home amount.

What You'll Actually Take Home

Here's a reality that surprises some people: in a typical case, the injured claimant takes home somewhere between 35% and 50% of the total settlement amount.

That percentage varies based on the circumstances. If there were significant case costs—expert witnesses, extensive discovery, a long litigation—more comes out. Premises cases often involve higher costs than simpler injury claims because of the expert witnesses we discussed in Chapter 19. If subrogation or lien claims were substantial, more comes out. If there are insurance coverage issues where the available limits are less than the true value of your damages, that can affect the percentage as well.

Every case is different. But going in with realistic expectations about take-home amounts helps avoid disappointment at the end.

Timeline: Agreement to Check in Hand

In most cases, clients can expect to receive their final take-home check somewhere between thirty and sixty days after a settlement is agreed upon.

That accounts for drafting and negotiating the settlement agreement, signing and execution, waiting for the insurance company to issue the check, depositing and clearing the check, finalizing subrogation and lien negotiations, and preparing the final disbursement.

Some cases move faster. Some take longer. But thirty to sixty days is a reasonable expectation for a typical case.

After a Verdict

If your case went to trial and you won a judgment in your favor, the collection process depends on what the other side decides to do.

If they accept the verdict and decide to pay, the process looks like a settlement. The money gets collected, deposited, cleared, and disbursed according to the same general framework.

If they want to keep fighting by filing an appeal, things get more complicated. They may be able to get a court order "staying execution" of the judgment. In plain terms, that means they don't have to pay the judgment while the appeal is pending.

The court may require them to post an appeal bond—money set aside to guarantee payment if the appeal fails. But the appeal process can take years, and you won't see your money until it's resolved.

What Can Cause Delays

Several things can delay the closing process beyond the typical timeline.

Defense inserting new terms. Sometimes the defense tries to insert previously unmentioned terms into the settlement agreement—conditions that weren't part of the original deal. This requires negotiation to resolve and can slow things down.

Cases involving children. If the injured person is a minor, the settlement may require court approval. This process, called minor settlement approval, adds steps and time. Your attorney will explain what's involved if this applies to your situation.

Unresponsive subrogated carriers or lienholders. Your attorney needs final numbers from health insurers and lienholders before disbursing funds. If they're slow to respond or unwilling to negotiate, it creates delays.

Insurance company delays. Sometimes the insurance company simply takes longer than expected to issue the check. There may be no good explanation. It's frustrating, but it happens.

If your case is experiencing unusual delays, ask your attorney what's causing the holdup and what's being done to move things forward.

Multiple Defendants

If there's more than one party on the other side of your case, you might go through this process at different times with each defendant.

This is particularly common in premises cases. As we discussed in Chapters 8 and 9, fall cases often involve multiple potentially responsible parties—the property owner, the tenant, a maintenance company, and possibly a government entity. You may identify and pursue claims against several of them.

You could settle relatively quickly with one defendant while still fighting through litigation with another. A settlement with one party doesn't necessarily end the whole case.

This matters because you need to understand what any particular settlement means for your overall situation. Does settling with the property owner resolve everything, or are you still pursuing claims against the maintenance company? Will there be more money coming, or is this it?

Discuss this with your attorney before agreeing to any partial settlement. Make sure you understand whether the settlement ends the whole case or just part of it.

The Bottom Line

Settlement doesn't mean immediate payment. Expect thirty to sixty days from agreement to check in hand—sometimes longer if complications arise.

Your take-home amount will be less than the settlement number. Attorney fees, taxes, case costs, and subrogation or lien payments all come out first. In a typical case, you'll take home somewhere between 35% and 50% of the total settlement.

Once you sign the settlement agreement, you're done with that party forever. Make sure you're settling at the right time, with a clear understanding of your injuries and future treatment needs.

The closing process can feel slow after everything you've been through. But it's the final step in getting you fairly compensated for what happened. Your attorney will guide you through it and make sure everything is handled properly before you receive your check.

CONCLUSION

You now know more about slip, trip, and fall cases than most people who go through one.

You understand why these cases are different—why liability is contested, why comparative fault matters, why jurors are skeptical, why experts are often essential. You know how to find the right attorney and what to expect from the relationship. You understand fee structures, evidence preservation, the importance of medical treatment, and the complexities of subrogation and liens.

You know that cases involving government property have strict deadlines that can bar your claim entirely if missed. You know that multiple parties may share responsibility and that identifying all of them matters for your recovery. You know what settlement negotiations look like and what to expect if your case goes to court.

None of this makes you a lawyer. But it makes you something just as important: an informed participant in your own case.

The Partnership

Throughout this book, we've emphasized that the attorney-client relationship should be a partnership. Your attorney brings legal expertise, experience with similar cases, and the skills to navigate a complex system. You bring the facts of your situation, responsiveness when needed, and honest communication about everything that matters.

When both sides do their jobs well, fair results are achievable. Even in difficult cases. Even when liability is contested. Even when the insurance company fights hard.

The key is mutual understanding. Your attorney needs to understand your goals, your concerns, and the full truth about what happened. You need to understand the challenges of your case, the realistic range of outcomes, and the strategy for getting there. When that communication exists, you're working as a team toward a common goal.

This book exists to give you the foundation for that partnership. The more you understand, the better the questions you can ask, the more effectively you can participate, and the stronger your position becomes.

What Comes Next

If you've been injured in a fall on someone else's property in New Mexico, the next step is straightforward: talk to an attorney.

Bring what you have. The photographs you took. The incident report if you got one. The names of any witnesses. Your medical records or at least a list of where you've been treated. Information about your health insurance and whether you have Medicare or Medicaid.

If you don't have all of that, come anyway. An experienced attorney can work with what's available and help you fill in the gaps.

Don't wait. Evidence disappears. Witnesses forget. Surveillance footage gets recorded over. And if there's any possibility that a government entity is involved, the 90-day notice deadline under the Tort Claims Act starts running the moment you fall.

The consultation is typically free. Use it to learn whether you have a case, what the challenges might be, and whether the attorney is someone you want to work with. You're not committed to anything by having a conversation.

A Final Word

Falls can be embarrassing. The instinct to minimize what happened, to brush it off, to not make a fuss—that's natural. New Mexicans pride themselves on being tough and self-reliant.

But there's nothing weak about protecting your rights. If someone else's negligence caused your injury, you deserve fair compensation for what you've lost. Medical bills, lost wages, pain, disruption to your life—these are real losses. The legal system exists to address them.

You didn't ask for this. You were walking through a store, a parking lot, a restaurant, a sidewalk. You were going about your day. And then, because someone failed to maintain their property safely, you were hurt.

Taking action isn't about getting rich. It's about being made whole. It's about holding negligent parties accountable. And it's about making sure you're not left bearing the costs of someone else's failure.

This book has given you the knowledge to navigate what comes next. Now it's up to you to use it.

We wish you a full recovery—and a fair result.

APPENDIX A
QUICK ANSWERS TO COMMON QUESTIONS

This appendix provides brief answers to the questions we hear most often. For fuller explanations, see the referenced chapters throughout the book.

Do I have a case, or was it "my fault" because I wasn't watching where I was going?

Maybe both—and you can still recover. New Mexico uses comparative fault, which means the jury assigns a percentage of fault to everyone involved, including you. If you were distracted or not watching where you walked, that might increase your share of fault. But it doesn't eliminate your claim. Even if a jury finds you 30% responsible, you can still recover the other 70% of your damages—as long as the property owner was also negligent. The question isn't whether you share some fault. It's whether the property owner failed to maintain reasonably safe premises. See Chapter 8.

What if there was a warning sign (or cones), but I still fell—does that kill my claim?

Not necessarily. A warning sign is just another fact in the mix. If you saw the sign and disregarded it, that will likely increase your share of fault. But there are still questions to consider. Was the sign conspicuous enough? Was it positioned where people would actually see it? Was one sign sufficient for the area? And why didn't the property owner just fix the hazard instead of posting a sign? Warning signs don't provide absolute protection from liability. See Chapter 8.

What if there wasn't a warning sign—does that automatically mean they're liable?

No. The lack of a warning sign doesn't automatically establish liability, just as the presence of one doesn't automatically defeat your claim. It's another fact in the analysis. The property owner might argue they didn't know about the hazard, or that it was so obvious no sign was needed, or that you should have noticed it anyway. The absence of a sign may support your case, but you still have to prove the property owner was negligent. See Chapter 8.

What if the hazard was "obvious" (like ice, a pothole, a wet floor)—can I still recover?

Yes. In New Mexico, property owners have a duty to keep their premises safe even if the hazard is obvious. The fact that a hazard is visible or apparent does not bar your claim. That said, an obvious hazard may factor into comparative fault—the defense will argue you should have avoided something so clearly dangerous. But it's not an automatic defense that eliminates liability. See Chapter 8.

Who is legally responsible: the business, the property owner, the tenant, or the maintenance company?

Potentially all of them. Premises cases often involve multiple responsible parties. The property owner may have duties regarding the building and common areas. The tenant operating the business may have duties regarding the space they control. A maintenance company may have contractual responsibility for inspections or repairs. If a public sidewalk is involved, the municipality may share responsibility. Your attorney's job is to identify all potentially liable parties—and missing one can hurt your recovery. See Chapters 8 and 9.

What if I fell at an apartment complex—does it matter if I'm a tenant vs. a guest?

It affects whose duties are at issue, but either way you may have a claim. Common areas are generally the landlord's responsibility regardless of who you are. Inside a unit, the tenant is typically responsible—unless the hazard involves something the landlord was obligated to repair and failed to fix after being notified. As a guest, you may have claims against the landlord, the tenant, or both, depending on where you fell and what caused it. See Chapter 12.

What if I fell at someone's house (friend/neighbor)—do I sue them personally, or is it insurance?

You sue them personally. Their homeowner's insurance will typically defend them and pay any judgment or settlement, but the lawsuit is filed against your friend or neighbor, not the insurance company. Homeowner's policies may also have modest medical payments coverage that can help with immediate bills. But understand: if you pursue a liability claim, you're suing someone you know. Given the impact on your relationship, and the fact that these cases can be harder to prove in a residential context, you need to be sure it's worth it. That's a discussion to have with your attorney.

What if the fall happened in a parking lot or walkway—does that change anything?

Not fundamentally, but it affects who's responsible. Parking lots and walkways may be controlled by the property owner, the tenant, a management company, or even the municipality if it's a public sidewalk. The same liability principles apply—was there a hazard, did the responsible party know or should they have known, did they fail to take reasonable action? The investigation into who controlled the area becomes important. See Chapters 9 and 12.

What if the dangerous condition was temporary (spilled drink, tracked-in water, loose mat)?

Temporary hazards raise questions about notice and response time. Did the property owner know about the spill? Should they have known based on reasonable inspection practices? How long was it there before you fell? A spill that happened five minutes earlier may not create liability if there wasn't time to discover it. A spill that sat there for an hour almost certainly does. See Chapter 8.

What if the dangerous condition was long-term (broken step, uneven sidewalk, bad lighting)?

Long-term hazards are generally easier to prove because the property owner had more opportunity to discover and fix them. If a broken step has been that way for months, it's hard to argue they didn't know about it. Prior complaints, work orders that weren't completed, and maintenance records become key evidence. See Chapters 8 and 10.

What evidence matters most—and what should I do right now to protect the claim?

Photographs of the hazard are the most powerful evidence—take them immediately if possible. Get witness names and contact information. Report the incident and request a copy of any incident report. Ask the property to preserve surveillance footage. Get medical attention promptly. Save the shoes you were wearing. If time has passed and you didn't do all this, don't panic—work with your attorney to address gaps. See Chapters 1 and 10.

Do photos/video help, and how do we get surveillance footage before it's deleted?

Photos help enormously—they may be the only proof the hazard existed, since property owners often fix problems quickly after an incident. Surveillance footage can be critical, but most systems record over themselves within days or weeks. Your attorney sends a preservation letter demanding that footage be kept. If it's destroyed after proper notice, there can be consequences. But the letter has to arrive in time. Move fast. See Chapter 10.

What if nobody saw me fall—can I still prove what happened?

Yes, though it's harder. Your own testimony about what happened is evidence. Photographs of the hazard support your account. Medical records documenting your injuries and their timing help establish that something happened. Surveillance footage, if preserved, can show the fall itself. Cases succeed without eyewitnesses, but corroborating evidence becomes more important. See Chapters 1 and 10.

What if an employee "helped me up" or apologized—does that matter legally?

It depends on the exact words. A general expression of sympathy—"I'm sorry that happened to you"—is probably not an admission of fault, and trying to make it one may come across as overreaching. A specific acknowledgment—"I'm sorry I left that cord there"—is different and may be more significant. Like so much in these cases, context matters. Don't assume an apology wins your case, but do tell your attorney exactly what was said.

What if I didn't go to the ER right away, or I "walked it off" and got worse later?

Delays in treatment create challenges but don't necessarily doom your case. The defense will argue that if you were really hurt, you would have sought care immediately. Your attorney may need to explain why the delay occurred and bring in medical experts to connect your injuries to the fall. The longer the gap, the harder this becomes. If you're hurt, get checked out—even if it seems minor at first. See Chapters 1 and 13.

Can I recover for medical bills, lost wages, and pain—and what about future care?

Yes to all of these. New Mexico law allows recovery for past and future medical expenses, lost income, pain and suffering, loss of enjoyment of life, disfigurement, and more. If you'll need ongoing treatment, future medical costs are part of your damages. In serious cases, a life care planner may be needed to calculate lifetime care needs. See Chapters 13 and 15.

How are settlement amounts determined for slip/trip-and-fall cases in New Mexico?

Settlement values depend on several factors: the severity of your injuries, the strength of liability, the available insurance coverage, and how much fault a jury might assign to you. Medical expenses serve as a reference point, but subjective damages like pain and suffering also matter. Your attorney evaluates comparable cases and develops a realistic range. Premises cases often settle for less than similar car accident cases because liability is more contested. See Chapter 15.

What if the insurance company says I'm exaggerating or points to a pre-existing condition?

Expect this. Insurance companies routinely argue that claimants are exaggerating and that injuries are pre-existing. Pre-existing conditions don't bar your claim—you can recover for the extent the fall made things worse. But you need medical evidence connecting your current condition to the incident. Be honest with your doctors and your attorney about your medical history. Hiding a pre-existing condition is far worse than disclosing it. See Chapter 13.

How long do I have to make a claim—and what deadlines apply if it happened on government property?

For most claims, you have three years from the date of the fall to file a lawsuit. But if a government entity may be responsible—the city, county, state, a public school—the New Mexico Tort Claims Act requires written notice within 90 days. Miss that deadline and your claim against the government may be barred forever, no matter how strong it is. Don't wait to find out if government property is involved. Talk to an attorney early. See Chapter 11.

Should I talk to the insurance adjuster, give a recorded statement, or sign medical releases?

Be very careful. The adjuster's job is to pay you as little as possible, and everything you say can be used to reduce your claim. Questions about your shoes, your phone, whether you kept shopping afterward, your medical history—they're building a case against you. Once you have an attorney, let them handle communication with the insurance company. Don't give recorded statements or sign broad medical releases without legal guidance. See Chapter 4.

APPENDIX B
GLOSSARY OF TERMS

Actual knowledge. When a property owner or occupant genuinely knew about a hazard before your fall—as opposed to constructive knowledge, where they should have known. Actual knowledge can be proven through prior complaints, employee testimony, or internal communications.

Appeal. A request for a higher court to review the legal decisions made by the trial court. Appeals focus on whether legal errors occurred—they don't involve new testimony or evidence.

Arbitration. A dispute resolution process where a neutral decision-maker (arbitrator) hears both sides and issues a ruling. In Bernalillo County, certain smaller claims must go through mandatory arbitration before trial.

Case costs. Expenses paid to others to move your case forward—separate from attorney fees. Includes copying charges for medical records, filing fees, court reporter fees for depositions, and expert witness fees. In contingency cases, your attorney typically advances these costs and gets reimbursed from your settlement.

Claimant. The person making the claim—you, the injured party. Also called the plaintiff once a lawsuit is filed.

CMS (Centers for Medicare and Medicaid Services). The federal agency that administers Medicare and Medicaid. CMS sets rules about how injury settlements must account for Medicare's interests.

Common areas. In rental properties, spaces shared by multiple tenants or accessible to visitors—hallways, stairwells, lobbies, parking lots, sidewalks. Generally the landlord's responsibility to maintain.

Comparative fault. New Mexico's system for allocating responsibility among all parties, including the injured person. The jury assigns a percentage of fault to each party, and your recovery is reduced by your share of fault.

Compensatory damages. Money intended to compensate you for what you lost—medical expenses, lost wages, pain and suffering, loss of enjoyment of life, and similar losses. Distinguished from punitive damages.

Complaint. The legal document that starts a lawsuit. Filing the complaint opens an official court case with a case number.

Constructive knowledge. When a property owner should have known about a hazard, even if they didn't actually know. If reasonable inspections would have revealed the hazard, the law treats the owner as if they knew about it.

Contingency fee. A fee arrangement where the attorney's payment is a percentage of your recovery. If you don't recover anything, you don't pay a fee. Standard in personal injury cases.

Damages. The money you're seeking to compensate for your losses. Includes both economic damages (medical bills, lost wages) and non-economic damages (pain and suffering, loss of enjoyment of life).

Damages caps. Legal limits on how much you can recover. Under the New Mexico Tort Claims Act, damages against government entities are capped at specific amounts.

Defendant. The party being sued—typically the property owner, business, or other responsible party.

Demand. The initial settlement amount your attorney asks for. This is a negotiating position, not a valuation—the final settlement will typically be lower.

Deposition. A formal questioning session where a witness answers questions under oath while a court reporter creates a transcript. Depositions happen during the discovery phase of litigation.

Disbursement. The final distribution of settlement funds. Your disbursement statement shows everything that comes out—attorney fees, costs, subrogation, liens—and your take-home amount.

Discovery. The formal process during litigation where both sides must share relevant information. Includes written questions (interrogatories), document requests, and depositions.

Disfigurement. Permanent changes to your body from an injury—scarring, amputation, or other visible effects. A category of damages you can recover.

Duty of care. The legal obligation to act reasonably to prevent harm to others. Property owners have a duty to exercise ordinary care to keep their premises safe.

Expert witness. A professional with specialized knowledge who testifies about technical issues. In premises cases, this often includes safety experts (who explain whether conditions were hazardous) and medical experts (who explain your injuries and treatment).

Federal Tort Claims Act (FTCA). The federal law governing injury claims against the United States government. Requires an administrative claim within two years before you can file suit.

Franchise. A business arrangement where a local operator runs a location under a national brand's name. The franchisee (local operator) typically bears liability for premises conditions, not the franchisor (national brand).

Gross receipts tax (GRT). New Mexico's tax on business income. Attorneys must pay GRT on their fees, and this is typically added to what comes out of your settlement. Rates vary by location.

Hazard. A dangerous condition that creates an unreasonable risk of harm. Not every condition is a hazard—the analysis depends on context, the type of property, and what's normal for that environment.

Independent medical examination (IME). A medical examination conducted by the defense's chosen doctor. Despite the name, it's not truly "independent"—the doctor is hired by the other side.

Interrogatories. Written questions that must be answered in writing and under oath during the discovery phase of litigation.

Judgment. The court's official decision after a trial. A judgment in your favor means the defendant owes you money.

Letter of protection. A letter from your attorney promising to pay a medical provider from your settlement in exchange for treatment now. Used when health insurance isn't available or doesn't cover certain providers.

Lien. A legal claim against your settlement filed by a medical provider. The provider waits for payment but has an enforceable right to collect when your case resolves.

Life care planner. An expert who develops comprehensive plans for ongoing medical care and calculates lifetime costs. Used in cases involving severe, life-altering injuries.

Litigation. The process of pursuing a case through the court system. Begins when a lawsuit is filed and can include discovery, motions, mediation, trial, and appeal.

Loss of consortium. Damages available to spouses or children for harm to their relationship with the injured person.

Loss of enjoyment of life. A category of damages for activities, hobbies, and pleasures you can no longer participate in because of your injuries.

Mediation. A settlement conference with a neutral third party (mediator) who tries to help both sides reach an agreement. The mediator doesn't decide the case—they facilitate negotiation.

Medicare conditional payments. Payments Medicare made for your injury-related treatment that they're entitled to recover from your settlement.

Medicare set-aside. Money from your settlement set aside to pay for future injury-related medical care before Medicare resumes coverage. Required in certain circumstances for Medicare recipients.

Medicare Secondary Payer Recovery Act. The federal law giving Medicare the right to be repaid from injury settlements for treatment they covered.

Negligence. The failure to exercise ordinary care—doing something a reasonable person wouldn't do, or failing to do something a reasonable person would do. The basis for most premises liability claims.

New Mexico Tort Claims Act (TCA). The state law governing injury claims against state and local government entities in New Mexico. Imposes a 90-day notice requirement and damages caps.

Notice. In premises liability, notice refers to whether the property owner knew or should have known about a hazard. In government claims, notice refers to the formal written notice required under the Tort Claims Act.

Ordinary care. The level of care a reasonable person would exercise under the circumstances. The standard property owners must meet—though what's "ordinary" varies by context.

Pain and suffering. A category of damages for physical pain you've experienced and will continue to experience because of your injuries.

Plaintiff. The person who files a lawsuit. Once your case goes to litigation, you become the plaintiff.

Policy limits. The maximum amount an insurance policy will pay. Your recovery is usually capped at available policy limits, regardless of how badly you were injured.

Premises liability. The area of law dealing with injuries caused by dangerous conditions on someone's property. Slip, trip, and fall cases are a type of premises liability claim.

Preservation letter. A formal notice sent to responsible parties demanding that they preserve evidence related to your claim—surveillance footage, incident reports, maintenance logs, and similar materials.

Punitive damages. Money awarded to punish a defendant for particularly bad conduct—reckless, malicious, or willful behavior. Separate from compensatory damages.

Release. A legal document you sign when settling that gives up your right to pursue any further claims against that party. Once signed, you can never go back for more money.

Requests for production. Formal demands for documents during the discovery phase of litigation.

Safety expert. An expert witness who testifies about whether conditions were hazardous, what safety standards apply, and whether the property owner's practices were reasonable.

Sanctions. Penalties a court can impose for misconduct—including destroying evidence after receiving a preservation letter.

Settlement. An agreement to resolve a case without trial. The defendant (or their insurance company) pays an agreed amount, and you release all claims.

Settlement agreement. The legal contract that documents the terms of a settlement. Includes the amount, the release of claims, and other terms.

Sovereign immunity. The legal doctrine that protects government entities from being sued. The Tort Claims Act waives sovereign immunity for certain types of claims, including many premises liability cases.

Statute of limitations. The deadline for filing a lawsuit. In New Mexico, most injury claims must be filed within three years. Government claims have shorter deadlines.

Subrogation. Your health insurance company's right to be repaid from your settlement for injury-related treatment they covered. Subrogation amounts are often negotiable.

Trust account. A special bank account where attorneys hold client funds. Settlement checks are deposited here and must clear before funds can be disbursed.

Verdict. The jury's decision after a trial. A verdict in your favor means the jury found the defendant liable and awarded damages.

Waiver. A document you sign giving up certain legal rights. Waivers of liability are enforceable in New Mexico but only for risks inherent in the activity—not for a property owner's negligence in maintaining safe premises.

APPENDIX C
QUESTIONS TO ASK BEFORE HIRING A LAWYER

Use these questions when meeting with an attorney to evaluate whether they're the right fit for your case. Pay attention not just to the answers, but to how they answer—patience, clarity, and respect matter as much as the substance.

About Their Practice

- Do you regularly handle slip, trip, and fall cases—not just car accidents?
- How will you identify all potentially responsible parties in my case?
- Do you have relationships with safety experts you trust? What makes them effective?
- Who will actually be working on my case? Will it be you or someone else at the firm?
- Are you licensed in New Mexico? Do you have experience in New Mexico courts?

About Fees and Costs

- What is your fee percentage?
- Are your fees different if we file a lawsuit? If we go to trial?

- How are case costs handled? Do you advance them, or will I need to pay as we go?
- Will I receive a cost breakdown before settling?
- If I already have a settlement offer, will your fee be calculated on the total settlement or just the increase you achieve?

About the Process

- How will we know when it's time to settle?
- How do you advise clients who are unsure whether a settlement offer is appropriate?
- Walk me through the claims negotiation process.
- Walk me through what litigation looks like if we have to sue.
- How will you investigate this case?

About Communication

- How often will I hear from you or your office?
- Who should I contact if I have questions?
- How quickly can I expect a response?

About My Specific Situation

- Based on what I've told you, what issues do you see in my case?
- Are there concerns about liability or comparative fault?
- Does my fall involve any government property that would trigger Tort Claims Act deadlines?
- Do you see anything that might complicate my claim?

Red Flags to Watch For

Walk away if you encounter any of these:

- High-pressure tactics urging you to sign up immediately

- Confusing fee arrangements, especially fees that increase if certain events happen
- Guarantees or promises of specific results
- Dismissing or minimizing your legitimate questions
- Claims of special relationships with adjusters or judges
- Offers of money or gifts to sign with them
- They contacted you after your fall without you reaching out first

Yellow Flags to Consider

These aren't necessarily deal-breakers, but they may signal the fit isn't right:

- The attorney seemed rushed or inattentive
- Their explanations didn't make sense to you
- You felt like you were on different wavelengths
- They lacked confidence or clarity when you asked about premises cases specifically

After the Meeting, Ask Yourself

- Did I feel treated with respect?
- Did the attorney listen to my situation before jumping to conclusions?
- Will I be comfortable entrusting this person with a significant financial matter?
- Can I see myself working with this person for potentially years?

If you can answer yes to these questions, you may have found the right attorney. If you have doubts, keep looking.

APPENDIX D
QUESTIONS TO ASK YOUR LAWYER DURING YOUR CASE

Once you've hired an attorney, staying engaged means asking the right questions at the right times. Use these questions throughout your case to understand what's happening and participate in key decisions.

At the Start of Your Case

- What information do you need from me to get started?
- What should I do if the property owner's insurance company contacts me directly?
- How should I document my injuries and recovery?
- Is there anything I should avoid doing or saying while my case is pending?
- Are there any critical deadlines I should know about—especially if government property might be involved?

About Responsible Parties and Coverage

- Who are all the potentially responsible parties in my case?
- Have you sent preservation letters to make sure evidence is protected?
- What insurance policies might apply to my case?

- Are there any coverage issues we need to address?
- Has the insurance company accepted liability, or are they disputing it?
- What are the policy limits we're dealing with?

During Medical Treatment

- Should I notify you when my treatment changes or when I see a new provider?
- How do I handle medical bills that arrive while my case is pending?
- Is there anything I need to know about my health insurance and subrogation?
- Do I have Medicare, Medicaid, or other coverage that requires special handling?
- What happens if I need treatment that my health insurance won't cover?

About Case Progress

- What stage is my case in right now?
- What are the next steps?
- Is there anything holding up progress on my case?
- What's your current timeline estimate?
- Is there anything you need from me?

About Liability and Comparative Fault

- How strong is our liability case?
- What arguments is the other side making about comparative fault?
- Will we need a safety expert to establish that the condition was hazardous?
- Are there other experts we'll need—and what will they cost?

When a Settlement Offer Comes In

- What is the offer?
- How does this compare to similar cases?
- Do you think this is a fair offer?
- What are the risks if we reject this and continue?
- What costs will we incur if we keep going—especially expert witness fees?
- If we accept, what will my actual take-home amount be after fees, costs, and subrogation?

If Litigation Becomes Necessary

- Why do you recommend filing a lawsuit at this point?
- How will filing a lawsuit change the timeline and costs?
- What should I expect during discovery?
- How should I prepare for my deposition?
- What are the realistic outcomes if this goes to trial?

Before Settling

- Are all my medical bills and records accounted for?
- Have we identified and addressed all subrogation and lien claims?
- Do I have any Medicare issues that need to be resolved?
- What will the final disbursement look like?
- Is there anything I should consider before agreeing to settle?
- Once I sign, is this truly final—no possibility of coming back for more?

General Questions for Any Stage

- Is there anything about my case I should be concerned about?
- Is there anything I can do to help move things forward?

- When should I expect to hear from you next?
- What's the best way to reach you if I have questions?

Tips for Good Communication

- Keep a list of questions as they come up so you don't forget them.
- When you contact the office, be specific about what you need.
- Respond promptly when your attorney's office contacts you.
- Keep your attorney informed about changes—new address, new insurance, new medical providers, changes in your condition.
- If something doesn't make sense, ask for clarification. There are no stupid questions about your own case.

APPENDIX E
WHAT TO BRING TO YOUR ATTORNEY CONSULTATION

Coming prepared to your first meeting helps your attorney evaluate your case and gets the relationship off to a strong start. Bring what you have—don't worry if you're missing some items.

About the Incident

- Photographs of the hazard and the scene
- Photographs of the location (address, street signs, business licenses on the wall)
- Incident report (if you obtained a copy)
- Names and contact information for any witnesses
- Notes about what happened, while your memory is fresh
- Any correspondence from the property owner or their insurance company

About Your Injuries and Treatment

- List of medical providers you've seen (names, addresses, dates)
- Medical records if you have them (your attorney can obtain these, but bring what you have)
- our health insurance card

- Your Medicare or Medicaid card, if applicable
- List of your current symptoms and how they affect your daily life

About Your Losses

- Pay stubs or documentation of missed work
- Receipts for out-of-pocket expenses related to your injury

Physical Evidence

- The shoes you were wearing when you fell (don't wear them to the meeting—bring them in a bag)

Questions

- Your list of questions for the attorney (Appendix C can help)

If You've Already Been Contacted by Insurance

- The adjuster's name, company, and contact information
- The claim number, if one was assigned
- Notes about what was discussed
- Any settlement offer you've received (in writing if possible)
- Any documents they've asked you to sign (don't sign anything before the consultation)

Don't Have Everything? Come Anyway.

If your fall just happened and you haven't gathered much yet, don't wait. If you've lost or never obtained certain items, don't let that stop you. An experienced attorney can work with what's available and help you fill in the gaps.

The most important thing you bring is your story. Be ready to explain what happened, how you've been affected, and what questions you have.

ALSO FROM 505 LEGAL

Follow the Money with New Mexico Public Records:
A 505 Legal Guide

Your tax dollars fund every government decision. This book shows you exactly how to find out where that money goes. No legal background needed. You'll learn to write effective records requests, handle delays and denials, and hold agencies accountable when they stonewall you. Whether you're tracking a city contract or investigating a state agency, this guide puts the power of transparency in your hands.

www.505legal.com

ALSO FROM 505 LEGAL

New Mexico Car Accident Claims:
A 505 Legal Guide

Car accidents are stressful enough without feeling lost in the legal process. This plain-English guide walks you through every step of a New Mexico car accident claim—from what to do at the scene to negotiating a fair settlement. You'll learn how New Mexico's unique insurance rules affect your case, what your claim is actually worth, and how to work effectively with adjusters and attorneys. No legal background required.

www.505legal.com

www.ingramcontent.com/pod-product-compliance
Lightning Source LLC
LaVergne TN
LVHW090603110826
845146LV00001B/247

* 9 7 9 8 9 9 2 8 3 8 1 4 5 *